AF291713

Wasteland

by Jason Haaf
and Scooter LaForge

I had to get away — away from Brooklyn, away from processing and reprocessing problems and solutions in my head. I had to get away from all of the waiting.

A beautiful young man, an Adonis, balanced the bottom of his feet on pool railings, dove in, and walked underwater looking like a zombie from John Carpenter's The Fog.

SKIN

Get Off

HANGING OUT

HONCHO

NATURAL MAN

FAN CLUB:

HOT SHOTS

TEN INCHES

In this bareness,
there is the opportunity
to show off at a public
pool for an audience
of two. You can walk
underwater while one
person, a sensitive type
from the city, watches
and wonders about you.

I'm sitting in the corner of a hotel bar because I wanted to see where I fit in all of this, inside of a gay hotel in Miami. Growing up in South Florida, in the 90s and 2000s, I missed out on a lot.

Unfamiliar with my feelings, I was stuck in space, stuck in my body. I want to see what may or may not happen tonight. I took a seat in the corner, opened my notebook, ready to write. The men here are staring. It's still early, and I don't know if I'm into it. I give another look and no, I don't think I am. Whenever I write in my notebook at a bar, it creates curiosity. But I knew that would happen, didn't I?

walk underwater
while one person
a sensitive type
from the city,
watches and
wonders about
you.

During the cab ride to the hotel, I thought of the men sunbathing nude at Haulover Beach, one who fluffed his cock while his lover walked up and down the shore looking for someone to play with. Before I packed up, the couple found two men who resembled themselves. The four of them stood in a circle, one with a full erection. It was like a bird puffing or fluffing its feathery chest in order to attract their mate, their bait.

As I wrote down my thoughts, a young blonde man walked over from the center of the bar, looked at my notebook and said, "I like your handwriting. It makes me feel safe."

Last night, I became mad or irritated and saddened by florida—again. Those feelings faded by midnight as I chatted about sex fantasies and kinks with someone back in New York

There were certain things with an artist that I wanted to avoid. When I met him, I wrote in my journal that he had tragedy written all over him. It sounds melodramatic, even severe in hindsight. His communication was as odd as it was erotic, sending me post-run videos of himself stripping down, but not all the way.

I'd receive videos of his hands. The camera slightly shook as he filmed his palm, the back of his hand, his palm, the back of his hand. I still don't know if I was meant to understand his private meaning.

My shoulders felt light, like I was 19. Push, pull, push, pull. I couldn't define him. And I know what happens to me when I cannot define. I go to every edge, every corner, every possibility.

Why do I know him? Why does he live in my head? Why do I want to get him out?

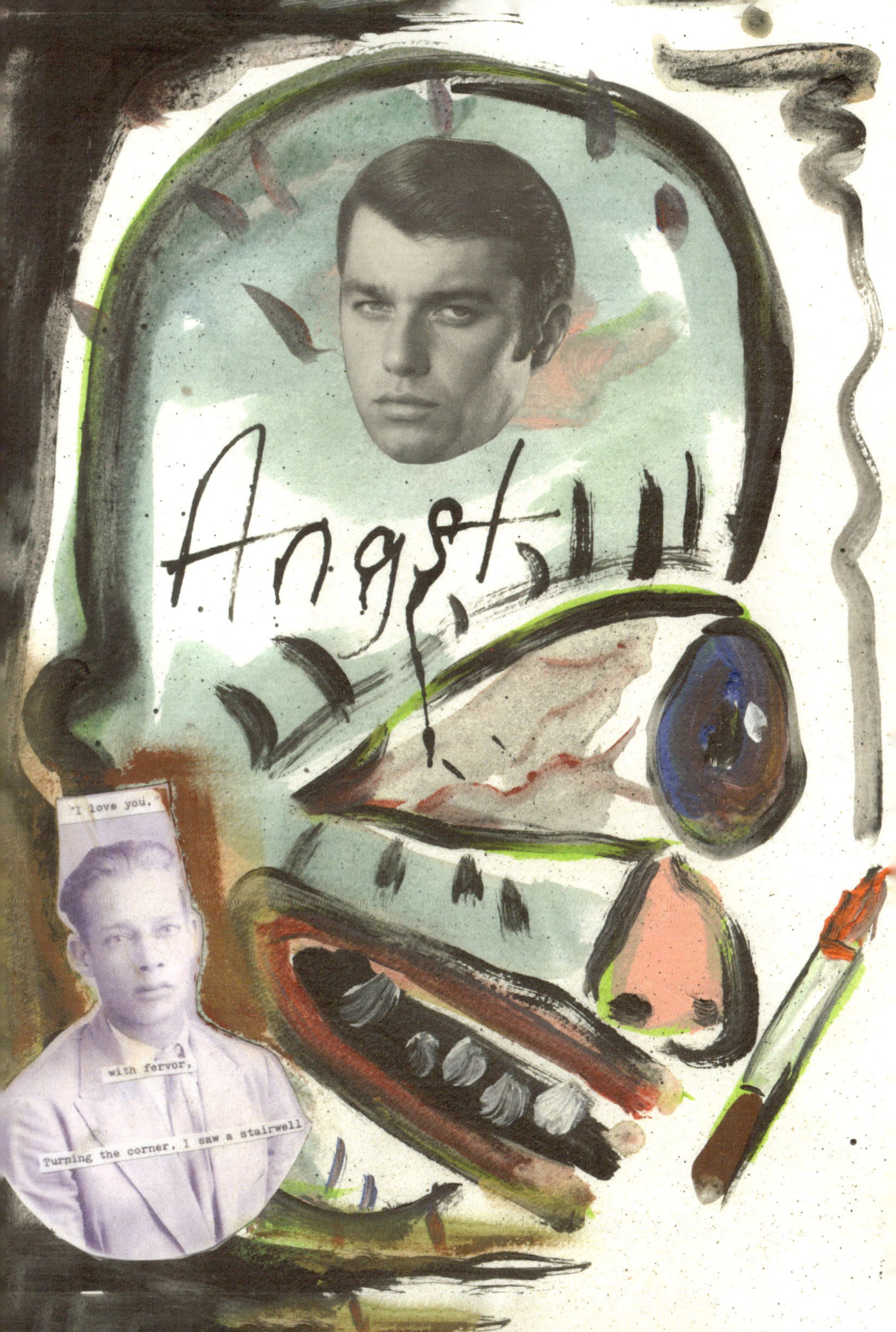

Angst.
"I love you,"
with fervor,
Turning the corner, I saw a stairwell

He was sitting next to me on the train, our knees touching. His leg is so much bigger than mine. Bobbing up and down, our pants made a swooshing sound.

"When do you want to hang out again?"

He wasn't another
stranger to avoid
a bag of mirages
I remember
Urgent art
relieved a heaviness

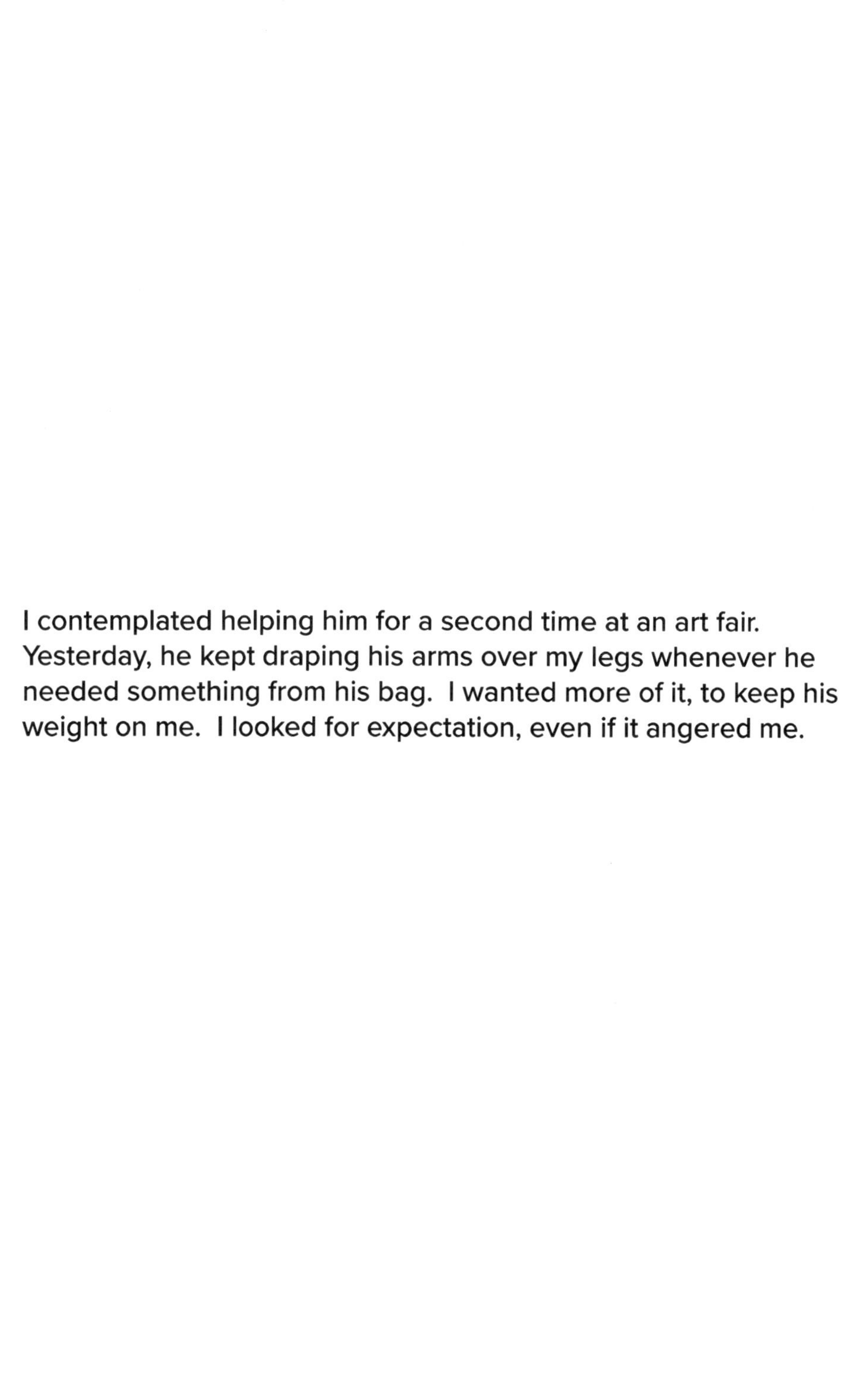

I contemplated helping him for a second time at an art fair. Yesterday, he kept draping his arms over my legs whenever he needed something from his bag. I wanted more of it, to keep his weight on me. I looked for expectation, even if it angered me.

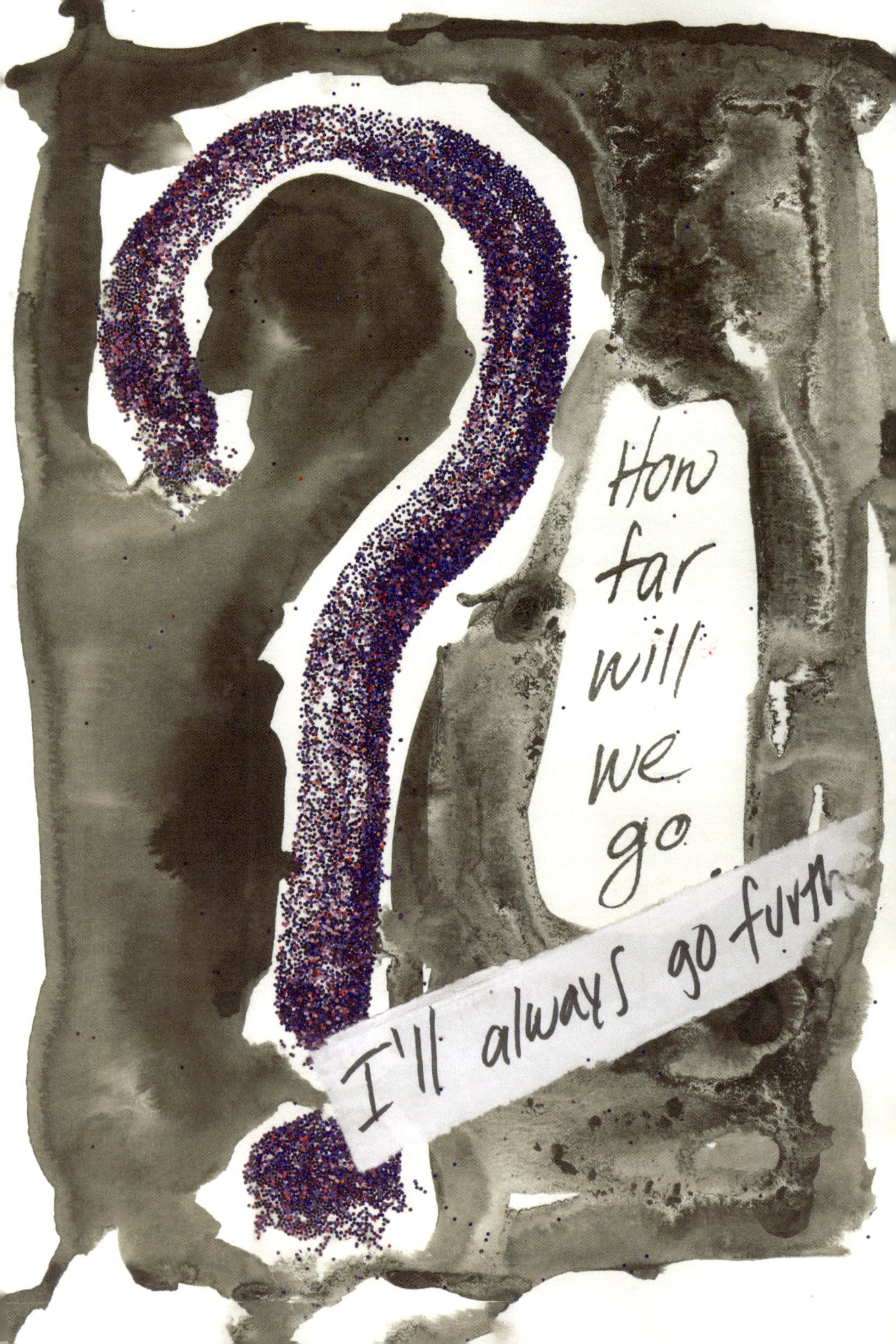
How
far
will
we
go
I'll always go furth

"I'm not really prepared to fuck you right now," he said.

"We don't have to have sex."

"I haven't been fucked in a long time."

"I just, at some point, I want to walk around with your cum in my stomach."

The artist and I were both nude, outside of his bedroom, his eyes directed at my chest. I wondered if he saw the gravity of age on my skin.

How can I tell
you who I am
(If I'm always
holding my breath)
Let it become
what it is

A week earlier, when we hugged to say goodbye, he didn't let go. "I don't know why I don't take advantage of you," he said.

My eyes widened.

"I mean, I know why. But I don't know. But I do…"

I wanted to kiss him, even though I felt like I was disrupting something. Instead, I held his head in my hands and kissed his temple.

"If you want to, you can," I said.

He rubbed his cheek against mine. Part of me felt lucky. I wanted a piece of him, but I didn't know what else to do. As I was leaving, I looked back, walking down the hall. The artist stood in his doorway, his head pointed to the ground.

Do friends kiss each other's
legs in bed?
Do they softly kiss
each other's foreheads
while laying on the other's
chest?

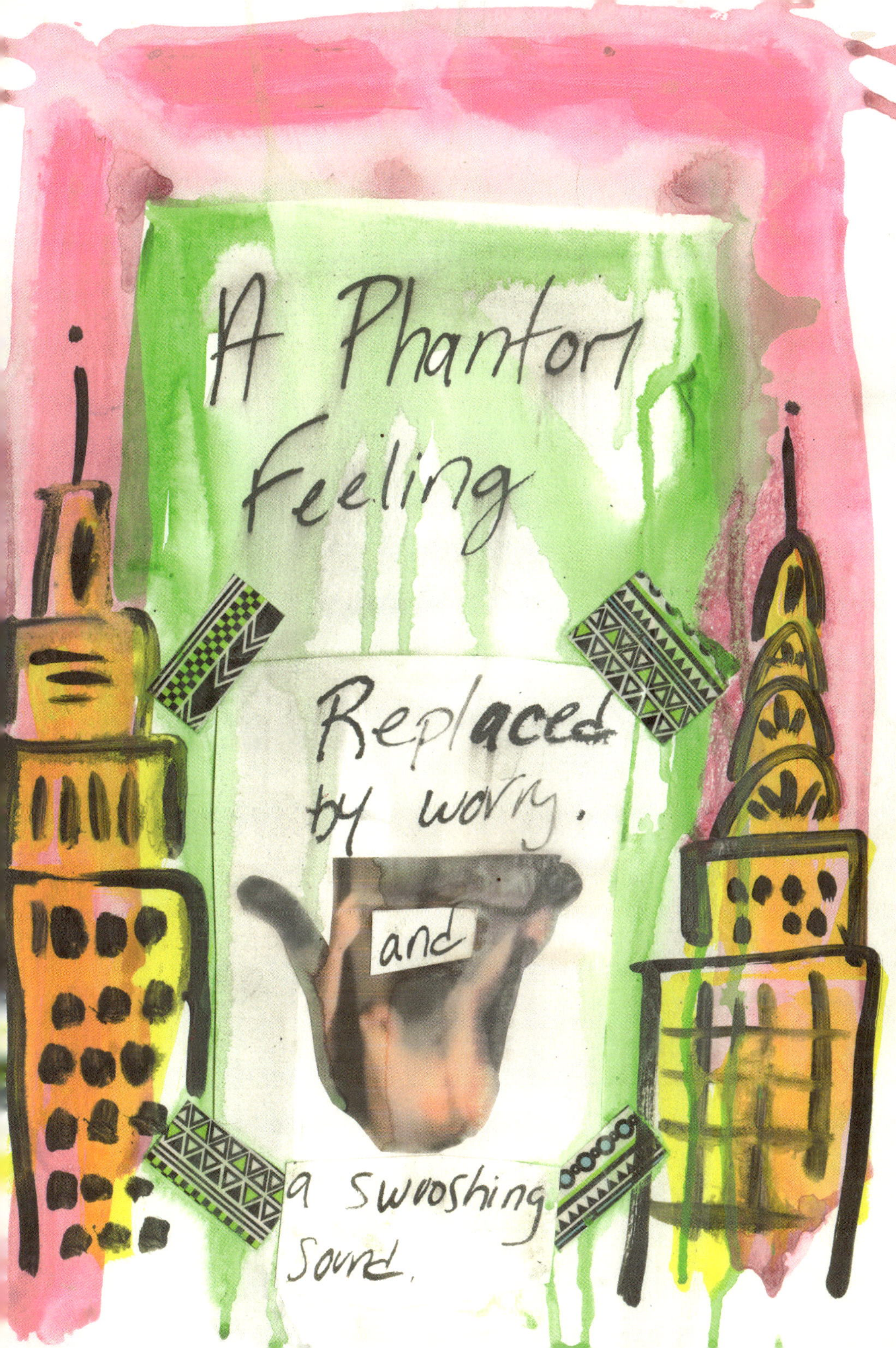
A Phantom
Feeling
Replaced
by worry.
and
a swooshing
sound.

I trust the first
thought I'll have
when I wake up.
I don't trust the rest
of the day chipping
it away.

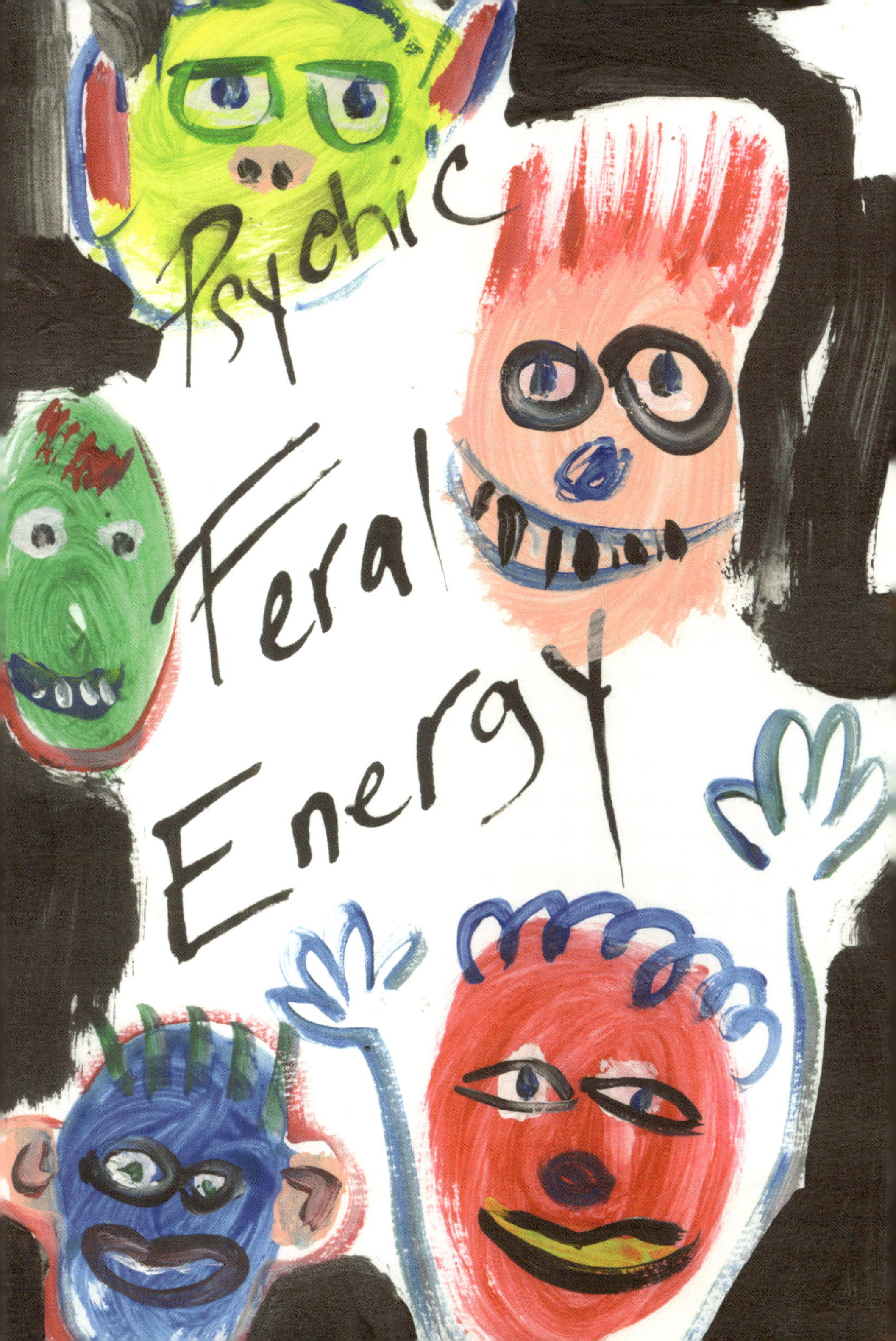
Psychic
Feral
Energy

I want

to keep

every option
keep every option
open

that's only in theory.

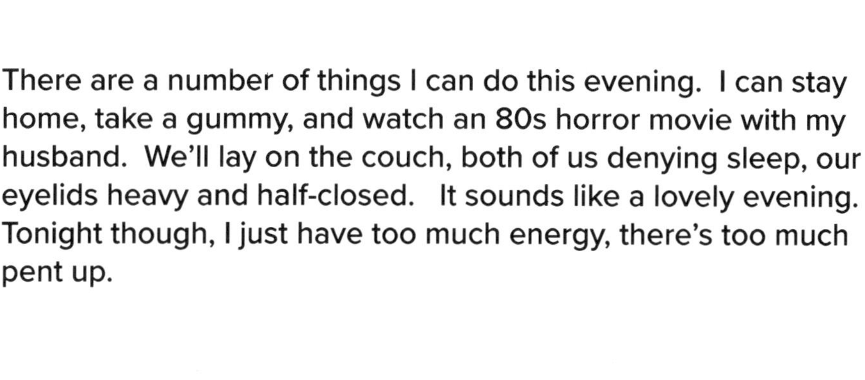

There are a number of things I can do this evening. I can stay home, take a gummy, and watch an 80s horror movie with my husband. We'll lay on the couch, both of us denying sleep, our eyelids heavy and half-closed.   It sounds like a lovely evening. Tonight though, I just have too much energy, there's too much pent up.

God is
restless
when
she's
alone

Like an animal carrying her young by their skin or cleaning off a mate or child, I have an urge to bite through skin, a shoulder, to press into a neck. It is an urge to smell a natural scent, to see sleep in one's eye when they wake.

What will it feel like to
feel my husband's body again?

Does the same current run
between us()

I miss him like how one
nurses their home.

A beautiful
young man,
an Adonis.

In this barrenness, there is the opportunity to show off at a public pool for ~~all~~ an audience of two.

walk underwater

CriSCO
Cris Place
our home.
place u here
queer angst
grows.
11th AVE
NYC
DiSCO
BET. 22nd & 23rd STS.

"Hold me," he said. I felt like I owed it to him.

I kissed him because I thought that's what he wanted me to do.

If I said too little, it would feel like an insult.

If I told him that I shared exactly who he was, it could be a breach of privacy.

I was a little nervous about time as I waited for my Lyft. Drivers kept switching, adding two or three minutes to my wait time. Today was the 2nd time I met up with Michael, Pulitzer Prize winning Michael.

"So, did you tell your husband you were coming here?" he asked.

"Yea I did. I said I was coming here."
"What did you tell him about me?"
DIAL NOW
I paused
1-900-963-6363
BILLED TO YOUR PHONE AS "REAL PEOPLE" $3.50 PER CALL
© COPYRIGHT 1989 REAL PEOPLE LTD.   YOU MUST BE 18 OR OVER

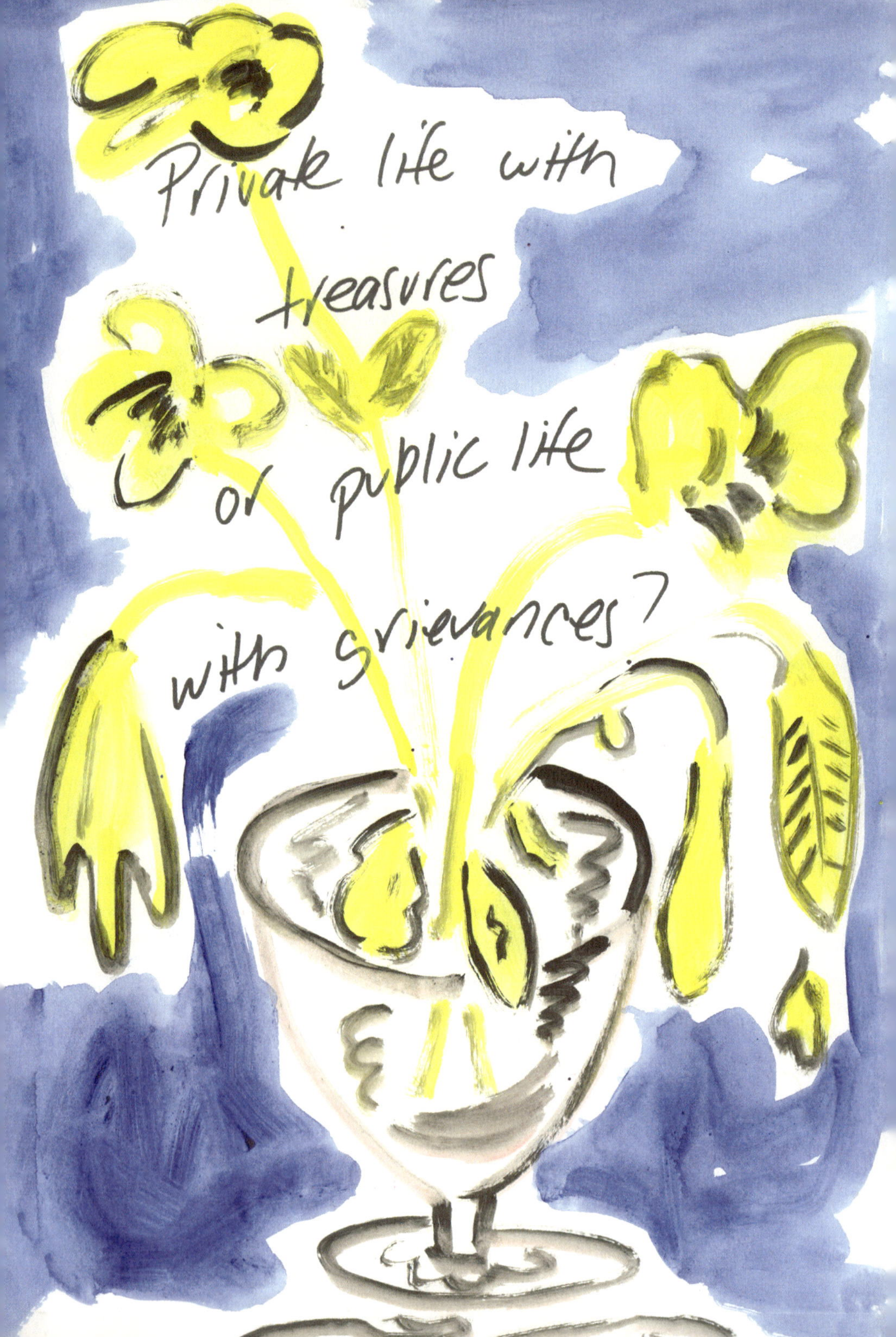

Private life with
treasures
or public life
with grievances?

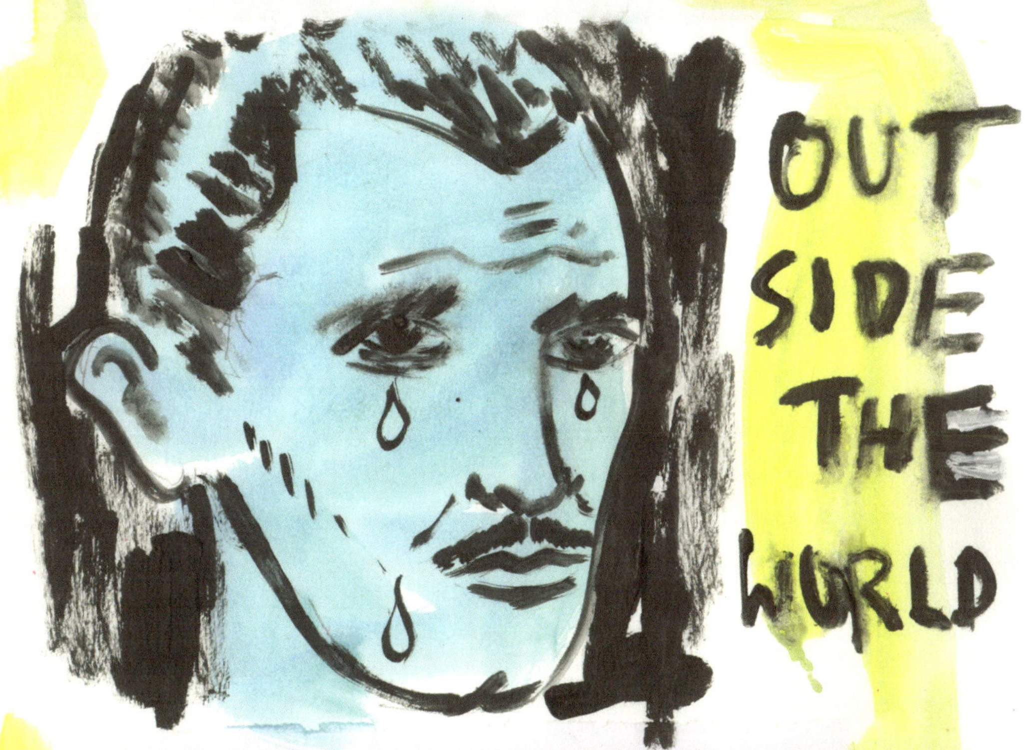

IS SO DANGEROUS
IT'S HARD TO
FIND SOMEONE
TO TRUST

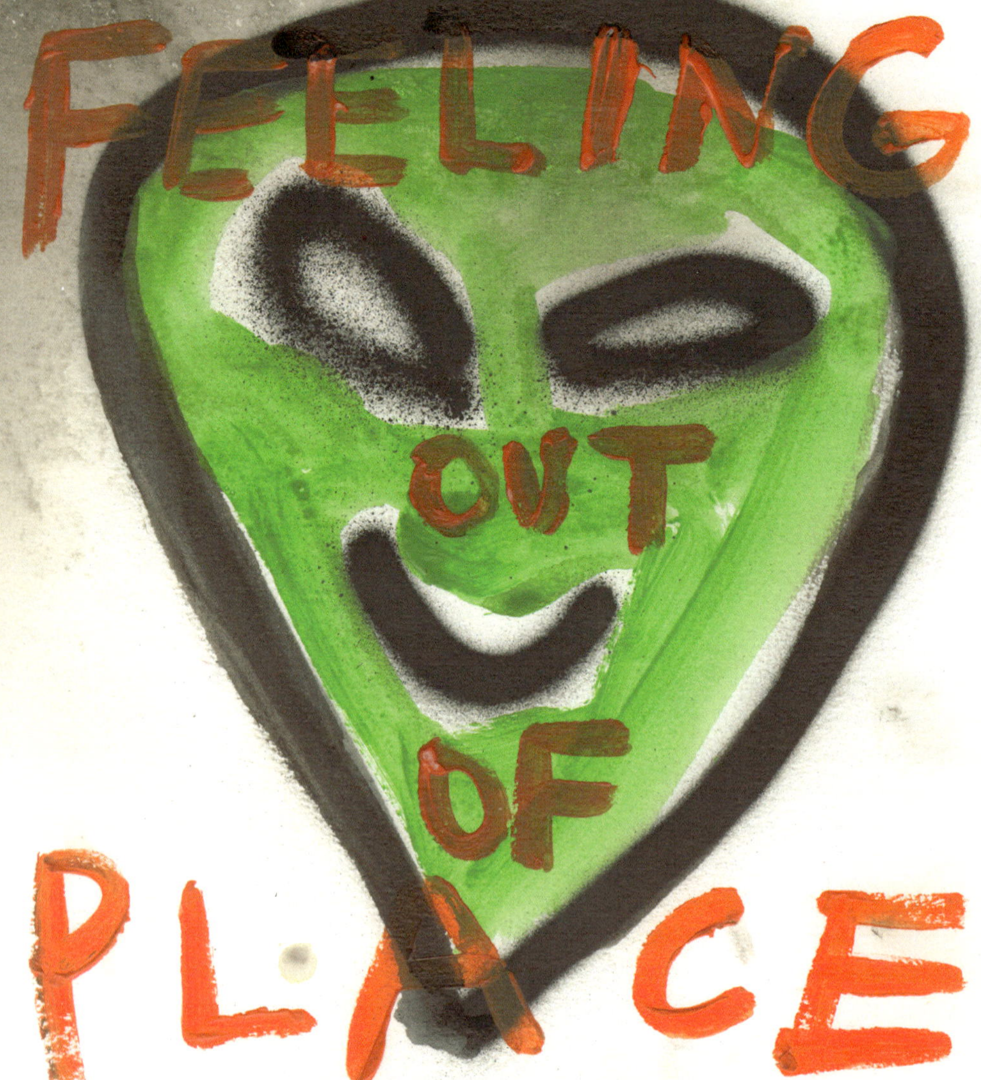
FEELING
OUT
OF
PLACE

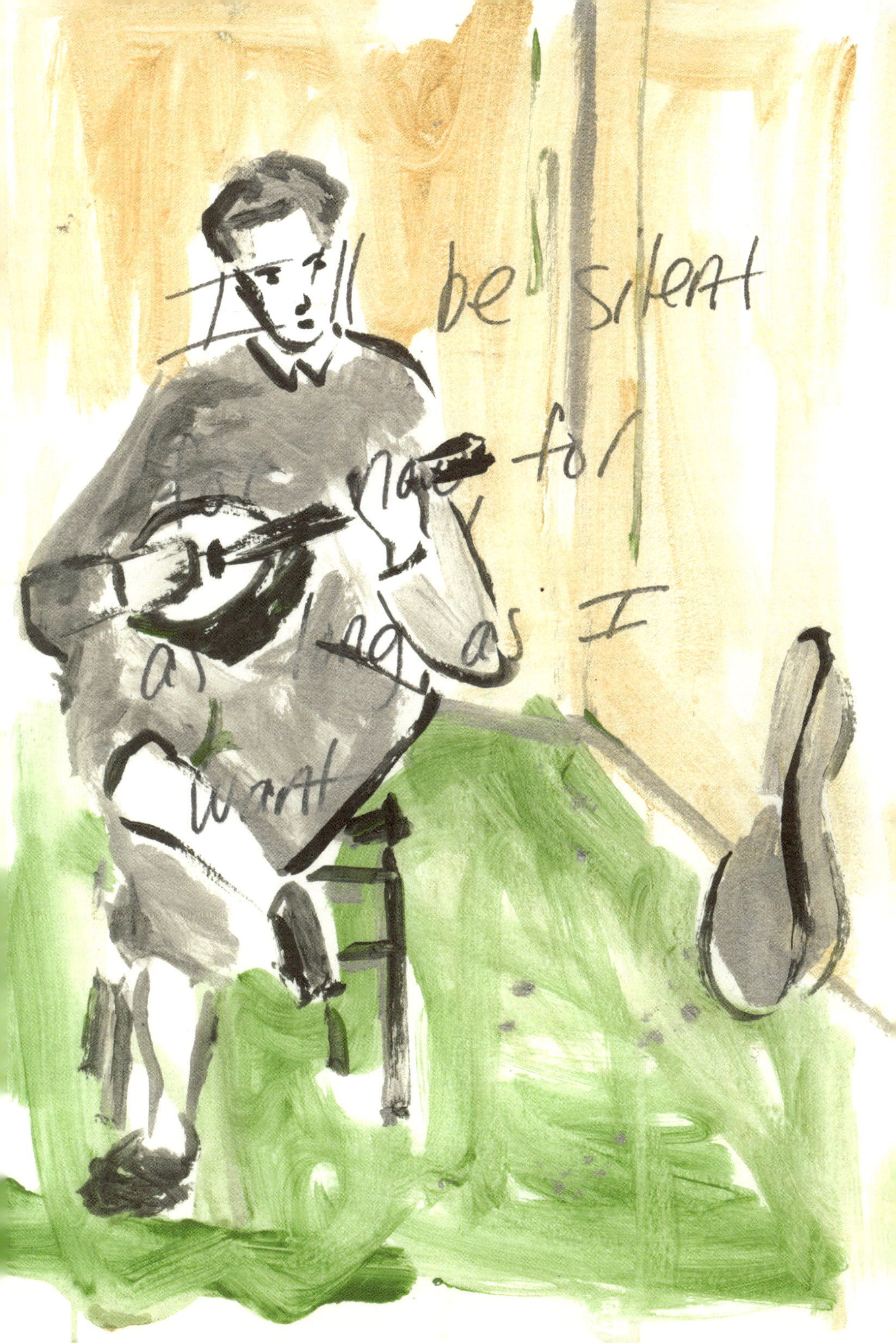
I'll be silent
for
as long as I
want

I collect strays—
both animals and people
I like knowing that they
come back. Is it because
survival is a necessity
or is it for me?

It feels tame right now. Yes, the world is on fire, but I've dulled my own flame. I was all fire last summer, running eight miles a day then chain smoking on the back porch. A romantic friendship was going to die, on its way to crashing because there was too much space between us, gaps filled with possibilities, scenarios and impossibilities.

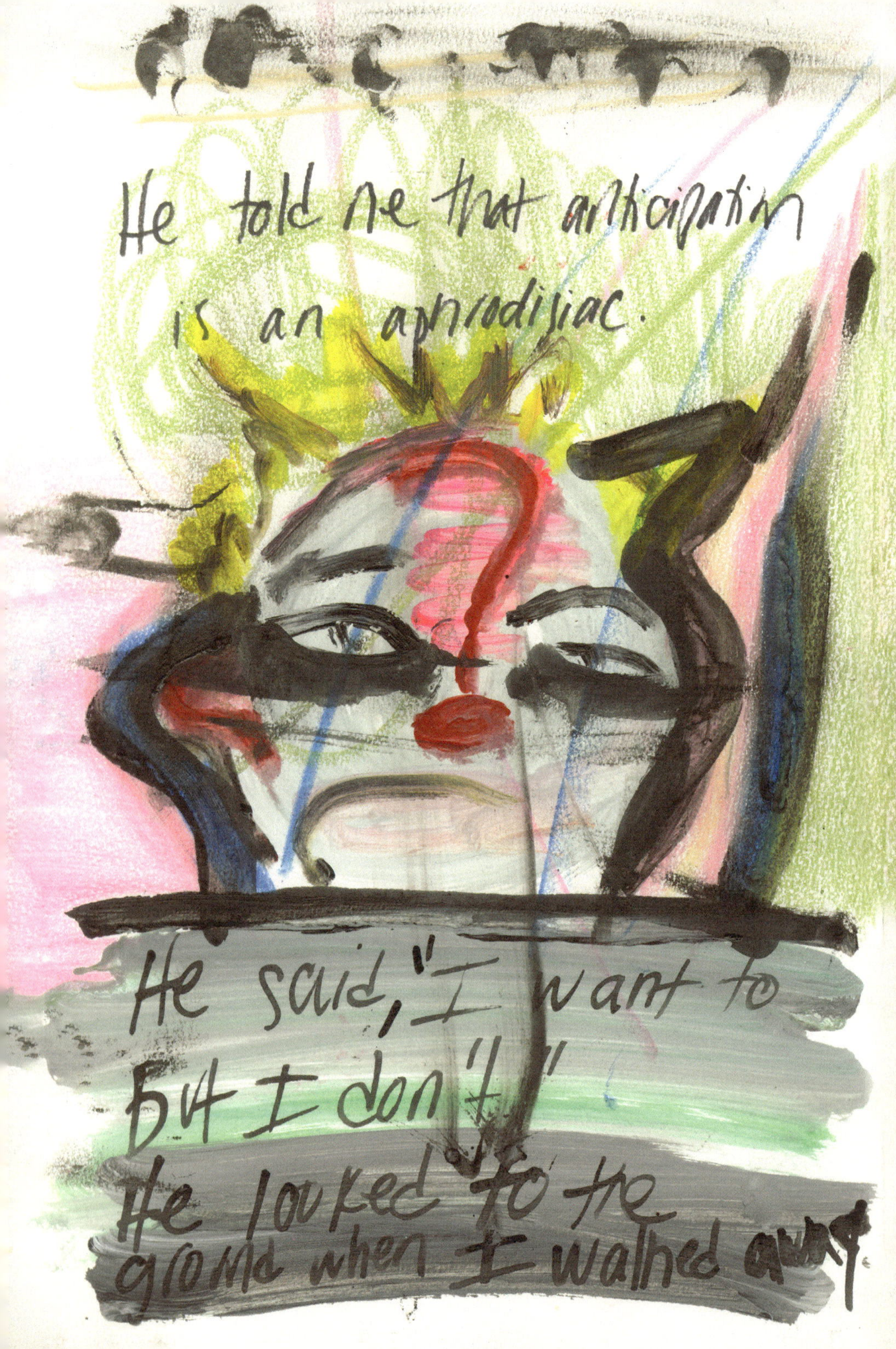

He told me that anticipation
is an aphrodisiac.

He said, "I want to
but I don't."
He looked to the
ground when I walked away.

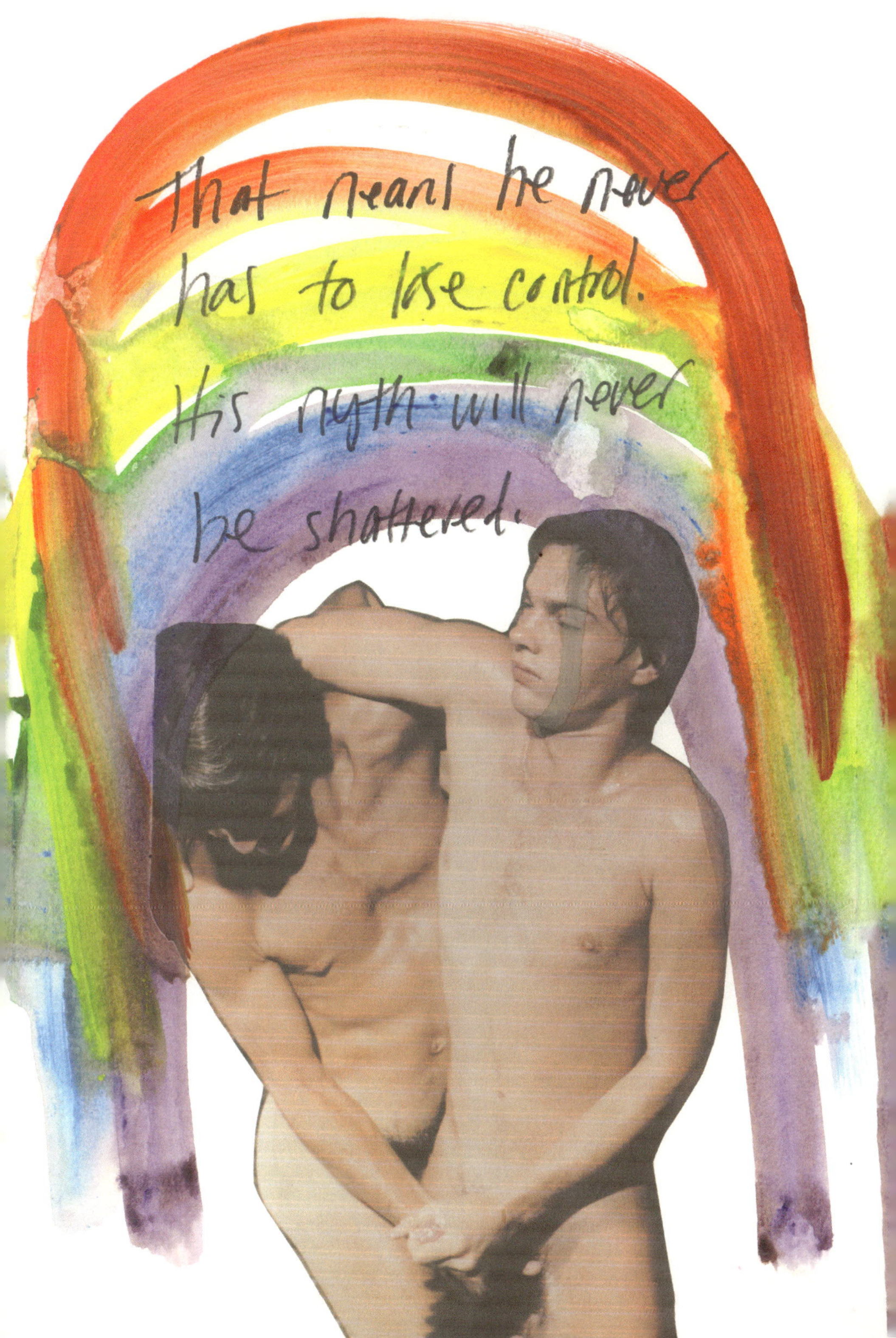

That meant he never
has to lose control.
His myth will never
be shattered.

Do friends
kiss eachother's
legs naked in bed

Do they kiss eachother's
foreheads while one lays
their head on the other's
chest for protection?

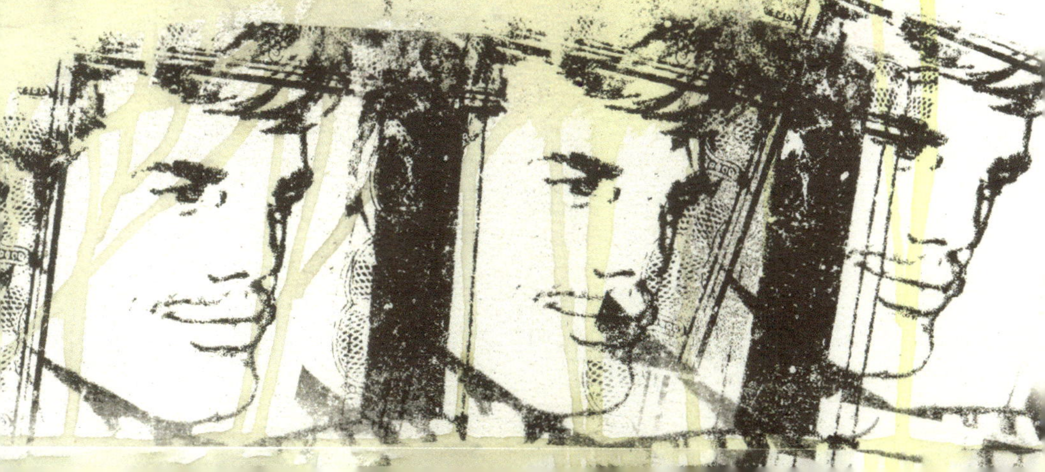

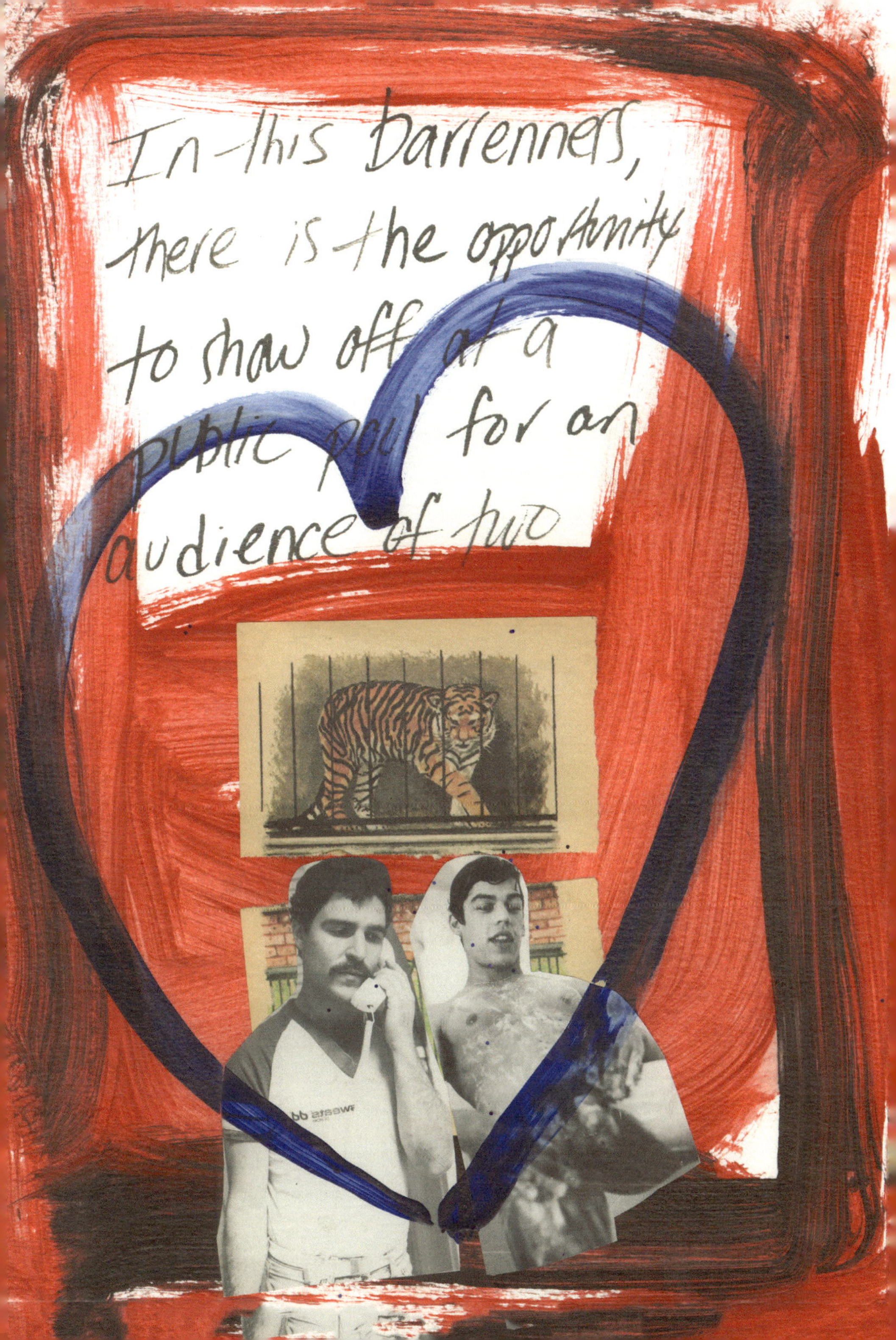
In this barrenness,
there is the opportunity
to show off at a
public pool for an
audience of two

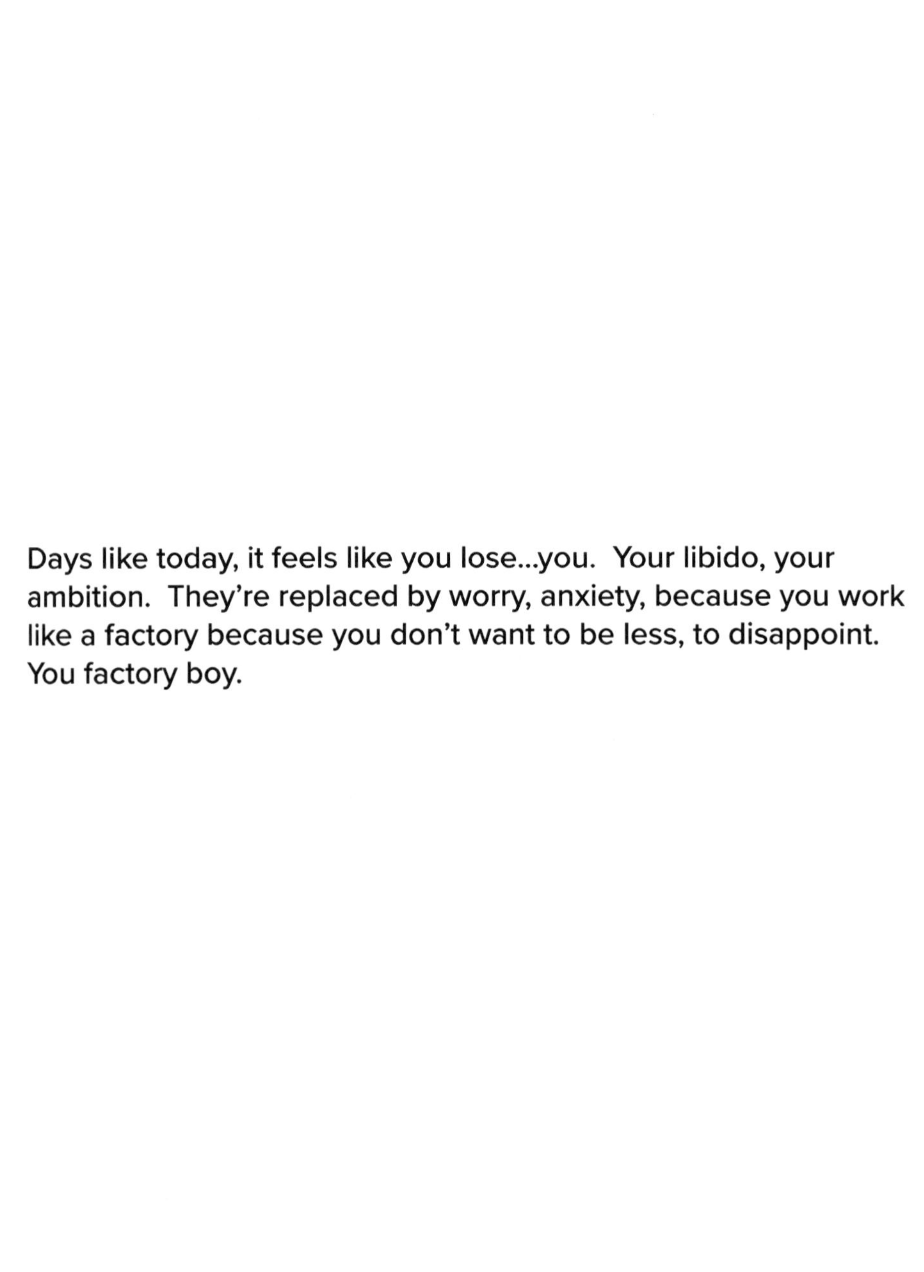

Days like today, it feels like you lose...you. Your libido, your ambition. They're replaced by worry, anxiety, because you work like a factory because you don't want to be less, to disappoint. You factory boy.

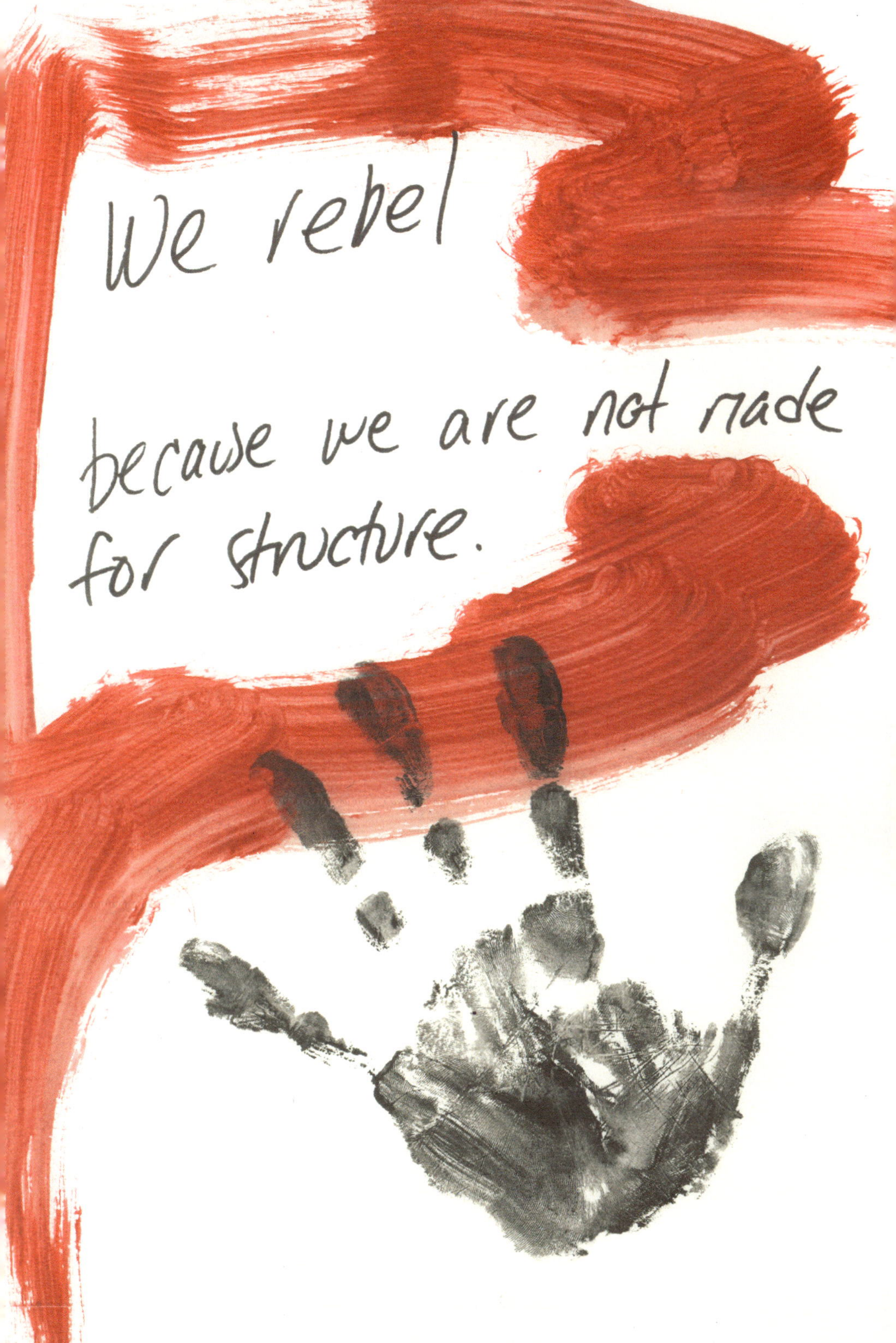

We rebel

because we are not made
for structure.

I'm not ready yet. I'm not ready to sip white wine on a balcony as a houseguest on Fire Island. I'm not ready to have a belly and thoughts of what never came to be. I'm not ready to watch videos and memes telling me of my own nostalgia from the 90's. I'm not ready to seek random cock as I sunbathe, ready to suck whoever comes my way, out of fear, out of a desperation for fruition.

I'm not willing to see someone from my past and say
to him, "it was my fault, too."
I look for peace in
synchronicities and in clock
radios. I find solace
and agreement in waiting
for another to finish their
sentence, because we share
roles of leading and follow-
ing one another. Sometimes,
I defend myself as a writer,
I defend it only in my head,
imagining that

Someone wants more of me than they really do. I've been seeing the same numbers in clocks and clock radios again. ~~that has~~ ~~to mean something good right?~~ It makes sense ~~for the~~ moment.

I took 2 sleeping
pills tonight. —
is isn't happening
again.
I don't care. This is
ot what reality
supposed to
It's not.

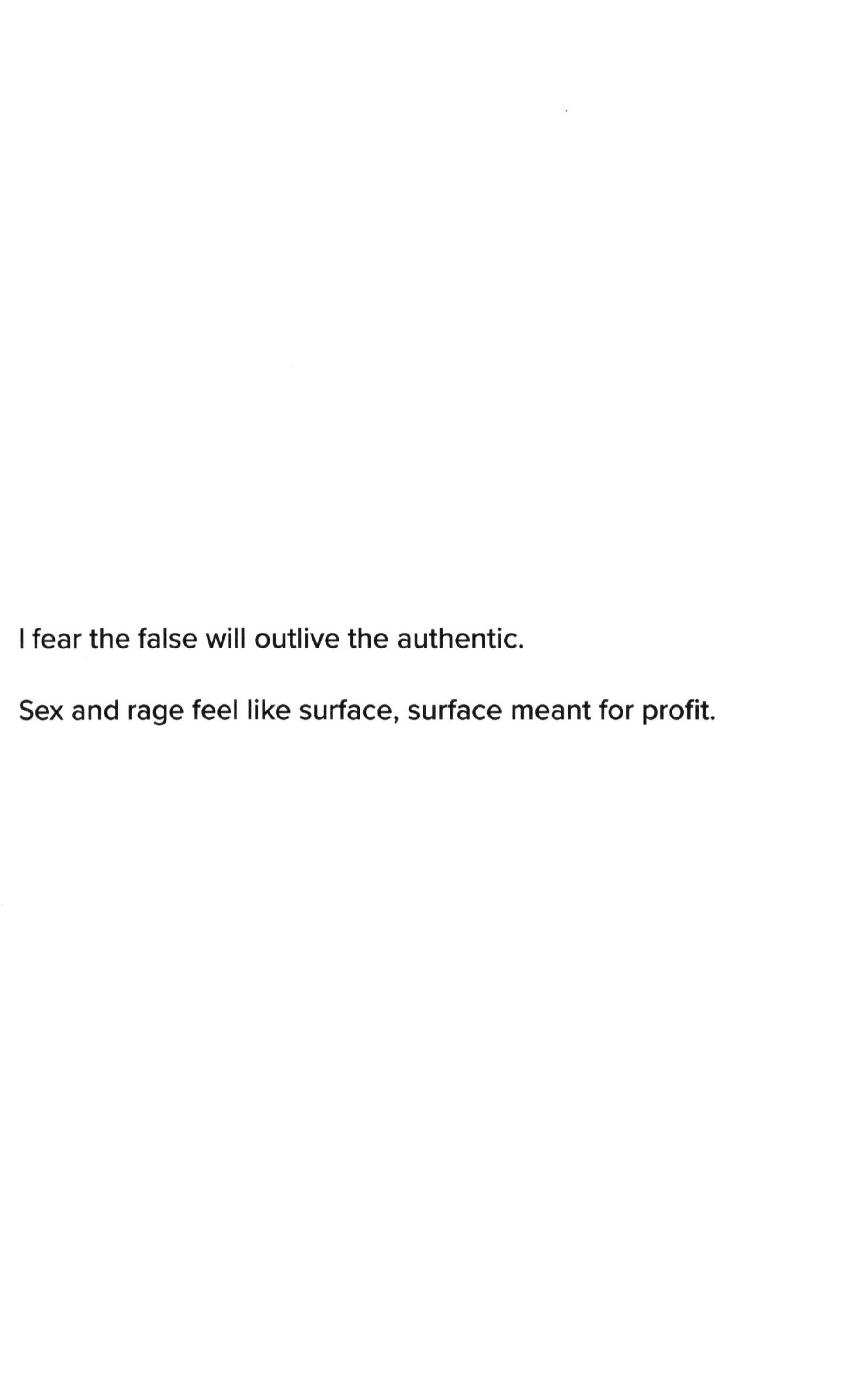

I fear the false will outlive the authentic.

Sex and rage feel like surface, surface meant for profit.

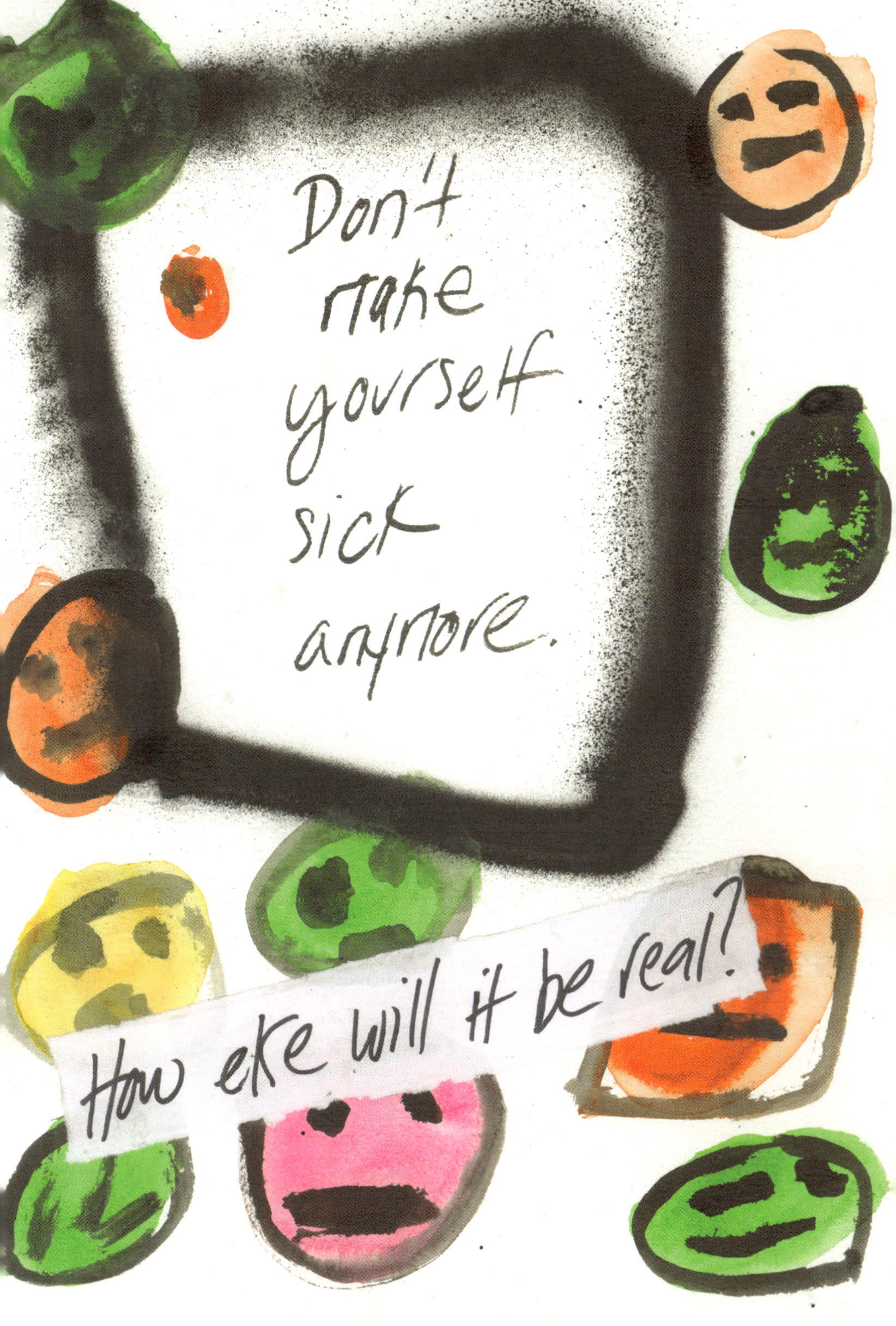
Don't make yourself sick anymore.
How eke will it be real?

I know I have to, or I should, take the next few days and sober up a bit, regulate my sleep, go running, and eat more consistently. I like how my voice sounds when it's free of nicotine. I want to be fresh and clear when I meet Robert, who I know lied about his age. I know because I had his phone number checked using White Pages online for $11.99.

Besides, older men sometimes lie about their age by five to ten years if they're over sixty. They can tell the truth with me, I like high numbers. I want to be next to, on, under a body older than mine, thicker than mine, hairier than mine, aged muscle protected by loose skin. To fuck or lay in their bed, in their always neat, sometimes stately apartments north of Times Square, to be sexualized and cared for by an older man, it's good for me, a sometimes son, a lover.

Even if an older man is strong and walks like a bulldog, there is wear in his strength that I find both calming and attractive. This morning, I asked Robert to send me a picture after I woke up very early, or went to bed late, or fell asleep after a gummy, passed out on the couch. He messaged a picture of himself, sitting at an outdoor table with a glass of wine, smiling, his face looking boyish yet filled with lines and creases. He told me to get some rest, and we'll talk soon. I let my cum run down my side and drifted back to sleep.

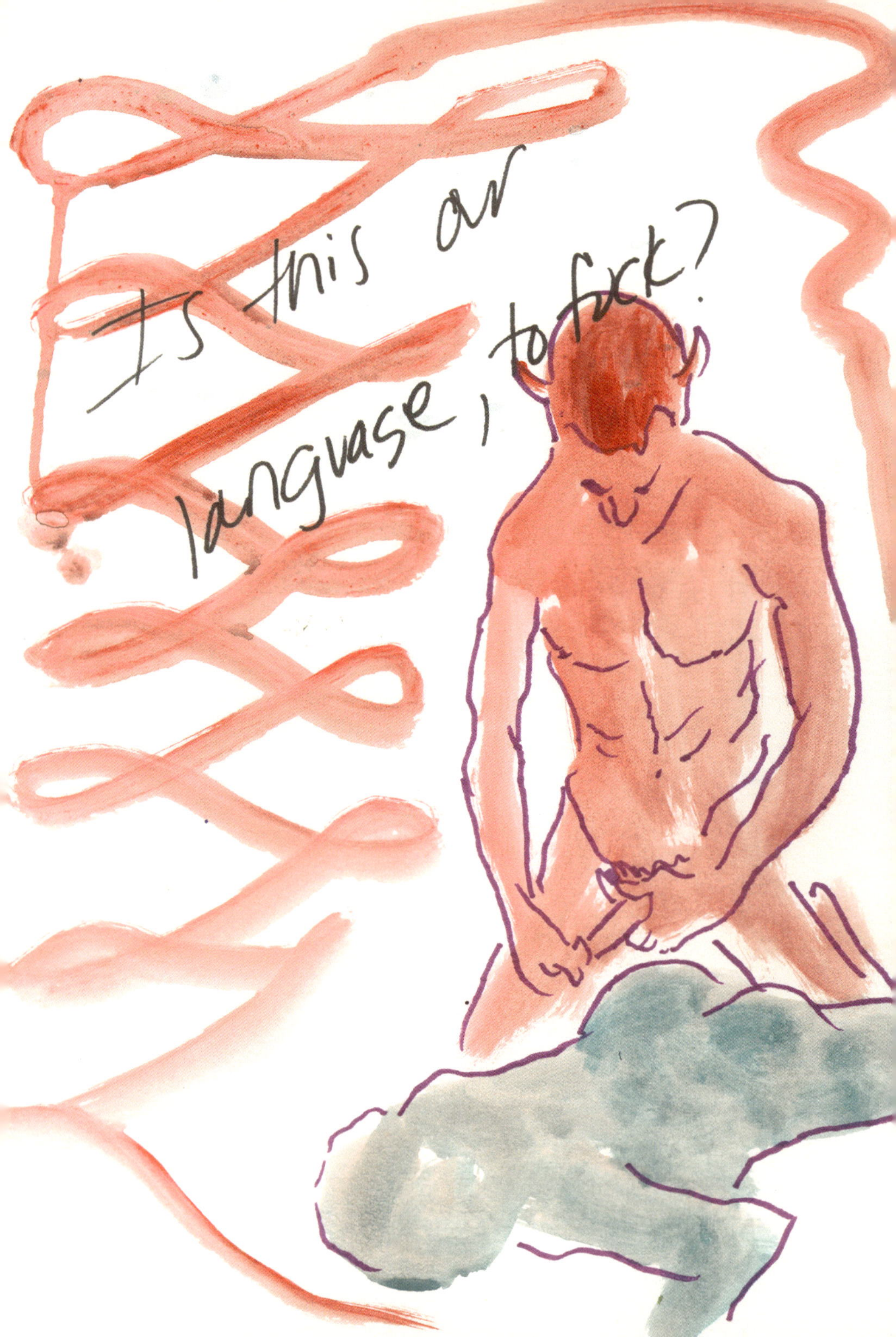

Is this our
language, to fuck?

What if this isn't sex?
what if it's language?
what is our source?
What is our kink?
How far will it go?
who is watching?
Were you always a pervert?
Did you wake up and expect not to be?
How much information can you store?
What if we never deleted our messages?

I wasn't supposed to touch him, not in the way that others did: mouths open, eyes glazed, in disbelief that their fantasy was coming true. My initial thoughts of flirting with an influencer were met with disgust. He paraded his body like a prize, one that didn't have to be earned, since he already decided to give it away. Then I, or we, discovered we shared the same kink.

He sits in a chair like a don, watching his husband phone fuck me. I try to make eye contact but my glasses are off and I can't see. I wrap my hands and feet into his partner and I tell them how good it feels.

They both tell me I'm safe, which is assuring and not something I've really looked for. This is transference.

My anxiety feels like weeds, like the dirt accumulating in our tub.
Cosmic flirtation
Leo looked a bit red from the motion of my mouth and hands.
Swinging and fucking
His shirt read Full Blown Chaos!

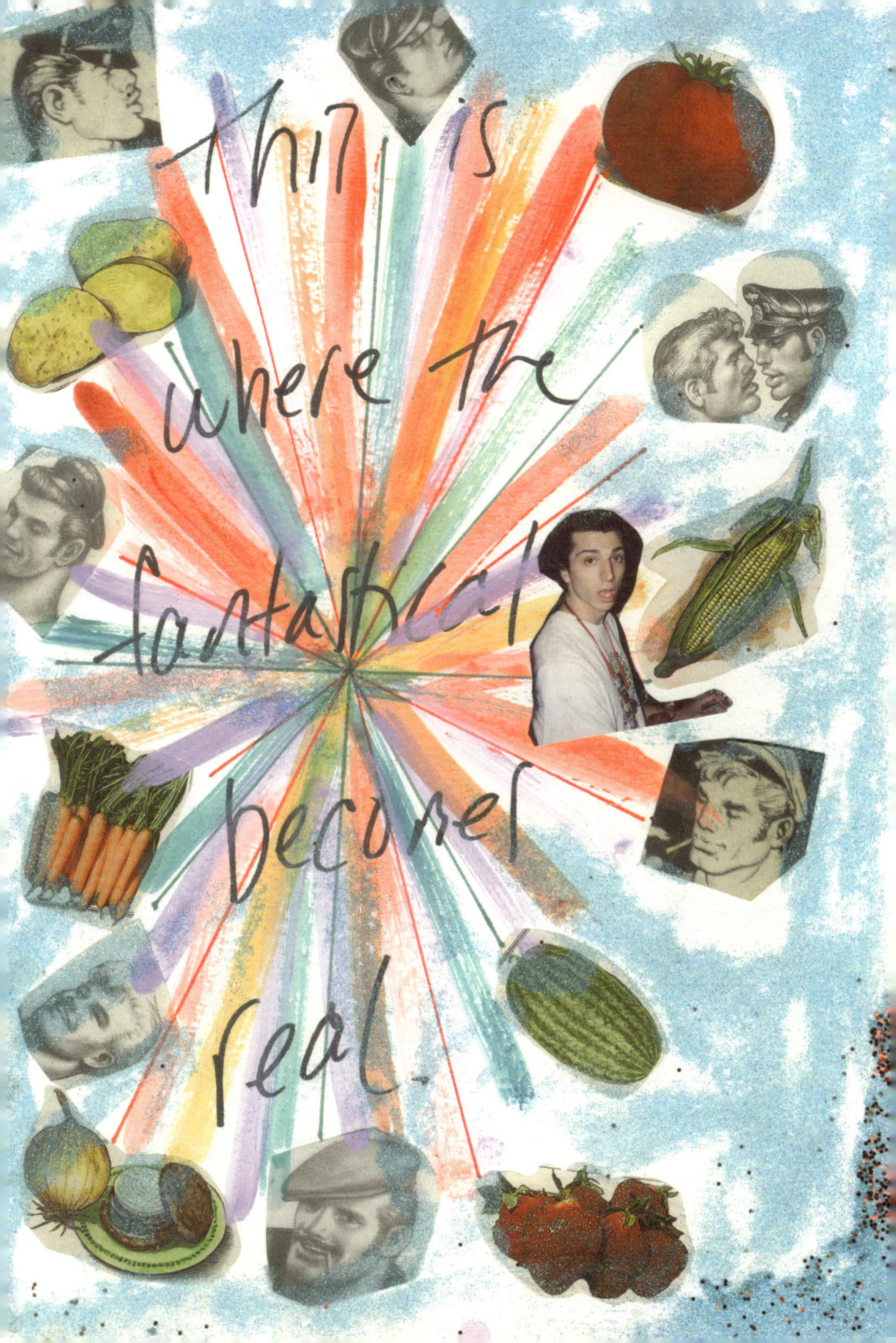

This is
where the
fantastical
becomes
real.

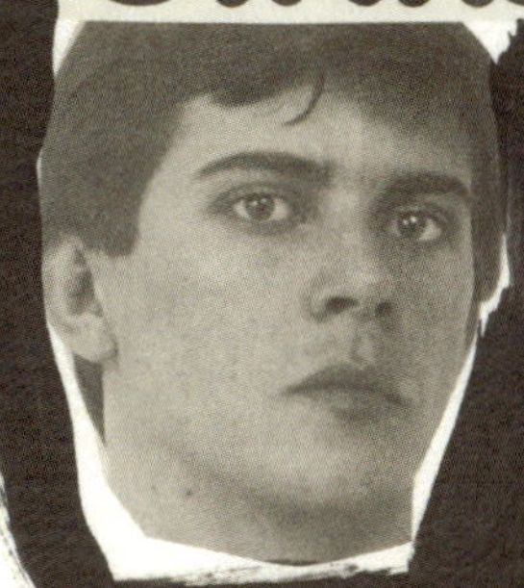

Share it
with a
stranger.

ZEUS

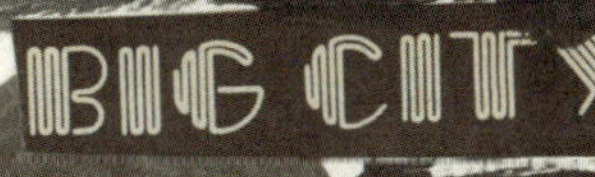

BIG CITY

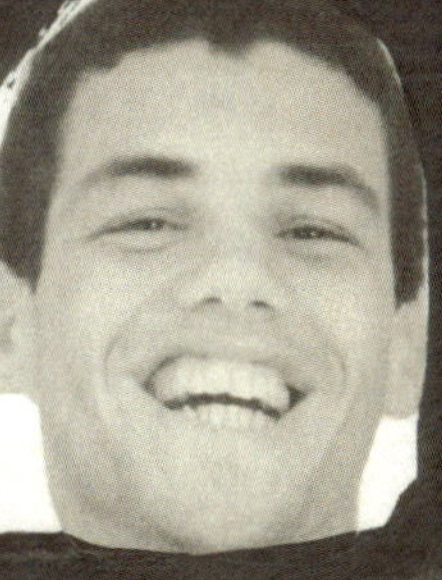

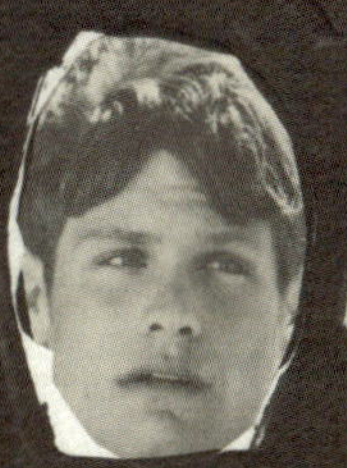

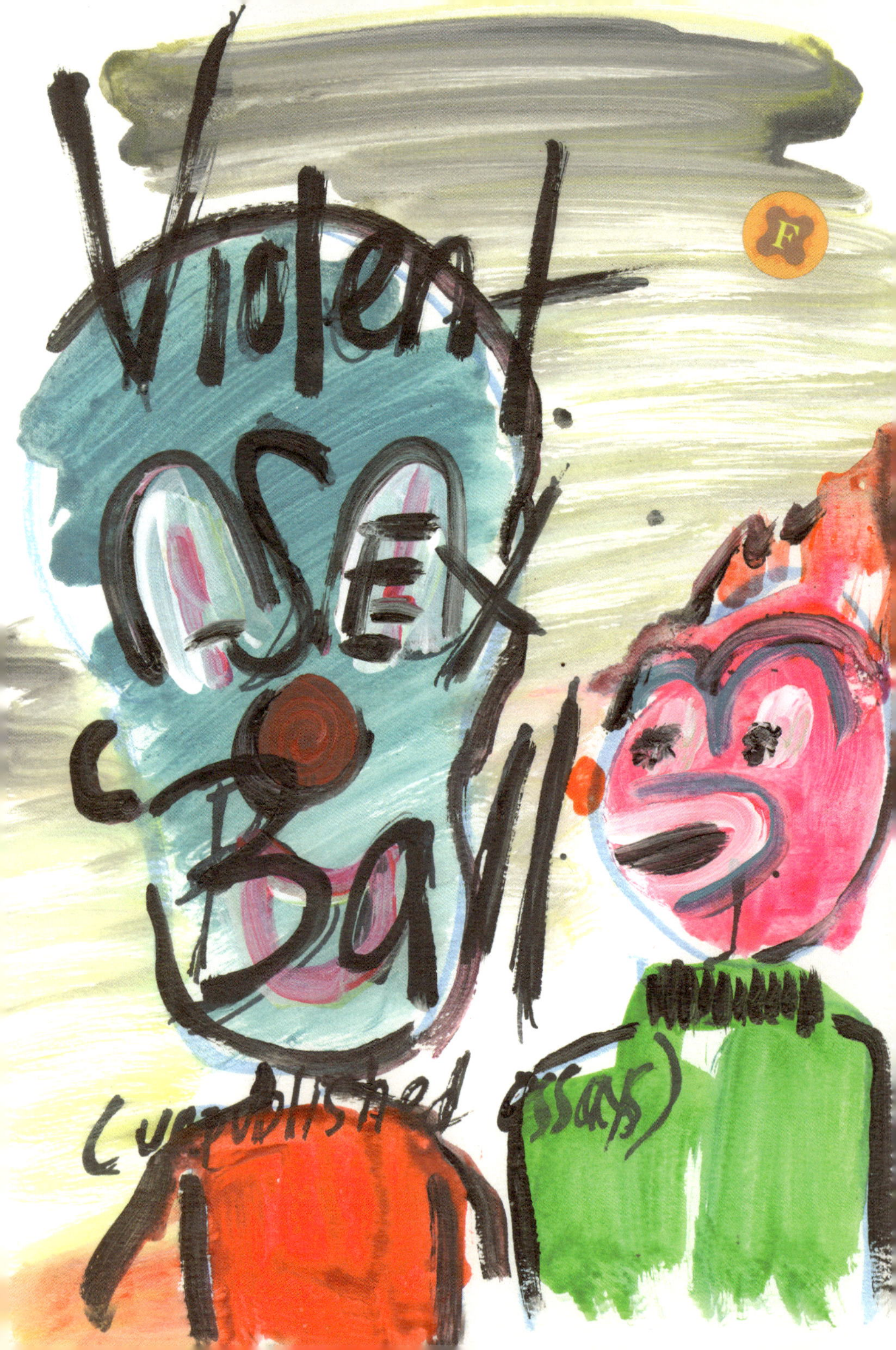

Violent
as a
Sex
Ball
(unpublished essays)
F

I push as far as I can, push myself, not getting any sleep, phone falling on my face watching porn, sending sexts, making plans for a foursome that may or may not happen. Drinking too much, going to a sex club, sucking a fat cock, getting my balls sucked while breathing poppers, passing out on the couch, more sexting, pushing limits with someone, tales of fantasy, of sex, violence, wanting to feel weird, strange, not quite myself, a release, sex, violence, screaming. Strangers online tell me they want no limits, all taboos. Violence, rape, incest, crying out, assholes beaten, leaking, stretched. Disgusted, turned on, I create a bond with them, all of them. They go to places with me and our communication lives in a secret room, a room where messages get deleted not long after our conversations end in cum.

These things.
These dynamics.
Disgusted, turned on.
"anticipation is an
aphrodisiac."

My senses
My sexuality
My kinks
are
all
connected
now

It can
feel
like
a burden

Bobbing

Intimacy is

ambition

diffusion.

Husband

Ji bido

If intimacy isn't shared

but then I'm a jealous diplomat

I watched the poet make our drinks, he splashed a bit of tap water into the glasses filled with tequila, sprinkled salt, and added a lime. It was really one of the best drinks I've had, as simple as it sounds. We sipped from our glasses and sat side-by-side on the sofa.

"You're cute in real life," he said.

"Thanks."

I wish he had not said that.

"It's true. You meet so many people who aren't what they present," he said.

"Sure."

He eyed my arms. "Can I ask about your tattoos?"

I pointed to the one on my upper left arm. It reads, 'A Trace of Exaggeration Remains.'

"It's a Rainer Maria Rilke quote. Actually, I see you have a book of his right there." I gestured to the book sitting on his coffee table.

"Oh, really, from which sonnet?" he asked.

I didn't know the answer. I remembered the full quote when I got the tattoo, many years ago, but now, I had no clue. "Oh, God, um, it sounds horrible, but I don't remember."

I picked up the book from the table and began rifling through it. For a second, I believed I would find where it was from. The poet looked at me with a kind of blank expression.

"You should know where your Rilke quote comes from," he said.

I didn't disagree.

What happens when I don't take on the weight for you?

"You sound brisque."
Yea, I said fuckin' brisque, what is that? I'n tellin' you ... all of the day. You ... a little too ... until ... you want on a ... no ... you who ... have ... brisque or shit. I can't ... "you sound brisque"—give me a break. I fuckin'
We're not starting over again.

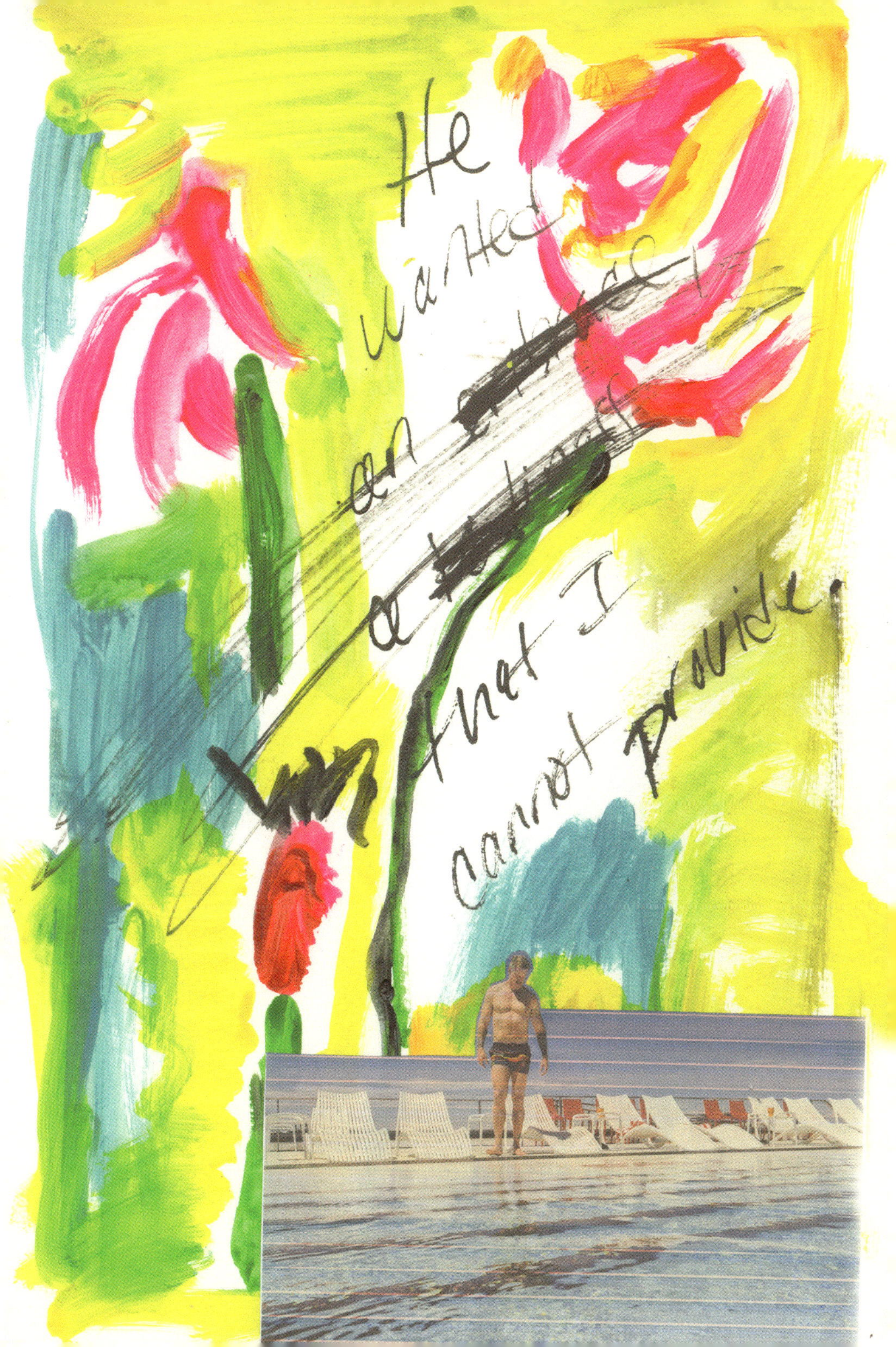

He
wanted
an
a that I
cannot provide

Rich wanted to hold me, to hold my hand even though he knew how much I hated PDA. I've always been best in my own space and when someone enters it, publicly, I feel exposed, as if I'm putting on a show. Unless it's in the written word, I don't perform for others.

He wanted an embrace, a loveliness which I was unable to provide.

"I'm trying my best to respect your boundaries," he said.

As we floated next to each other, I stretched my legs and felt rocky sand beneath my feet. I walked towards him. I walked into him. I may not love if someone tries to embrace me, but I can move towards them.   He put his arms around my shoulders and I carried him in the water, feeling a confidence that was mine. We stood in place and I saw an island not far in the distance. I thought of the act of writing and said to myself, *Words are a protest.*

Leaning into my ear, Rich said, "He really got into your head, didn't he?"

I've done
everything
I can to
know you and
to know your
silence. I've
put myself
in your
head for
4 years
And all
I see
is a black
reflection
of
yourself.

assert
assert
assert
yourself
and
smile.
smile
kindly

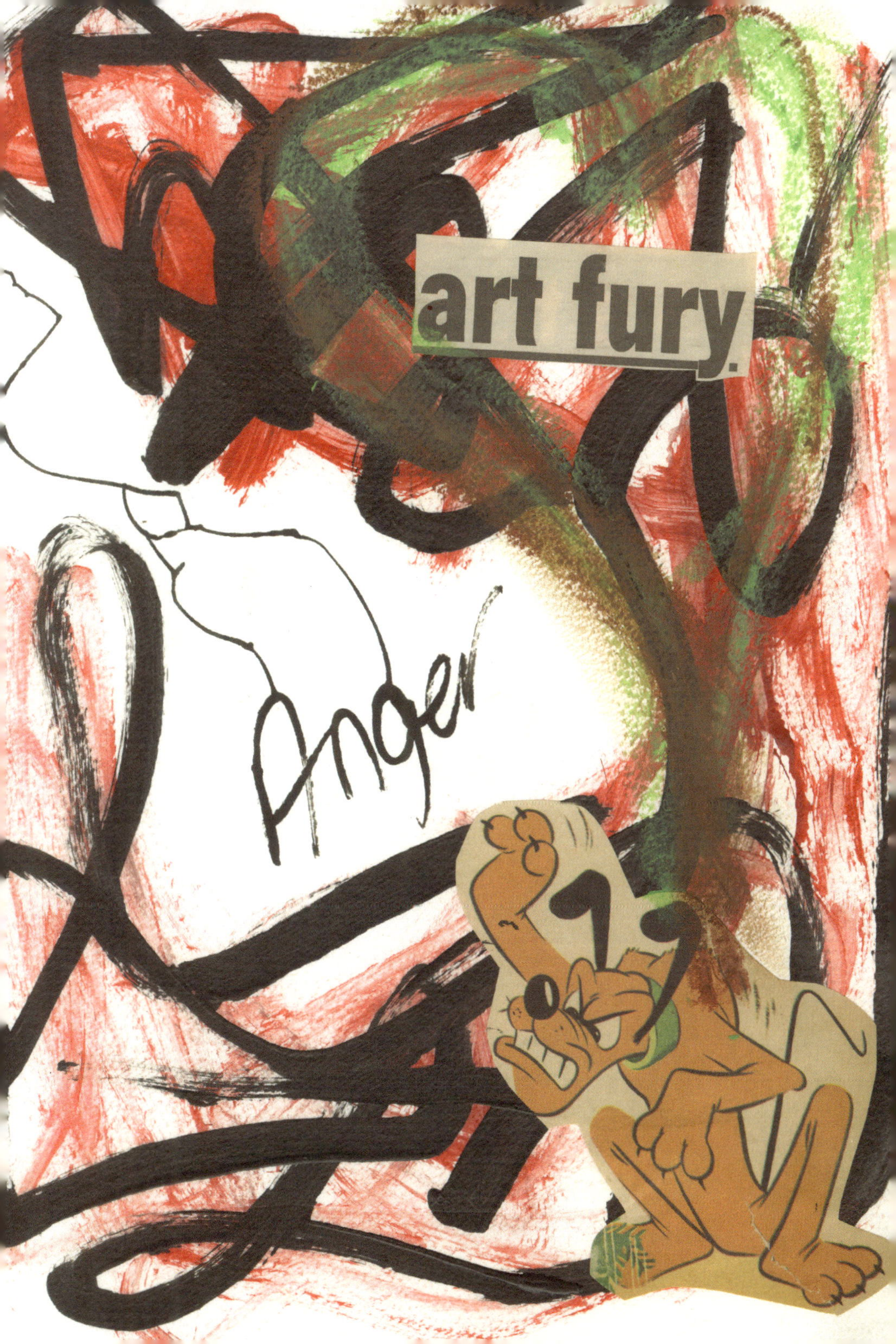
art fury.
Anger

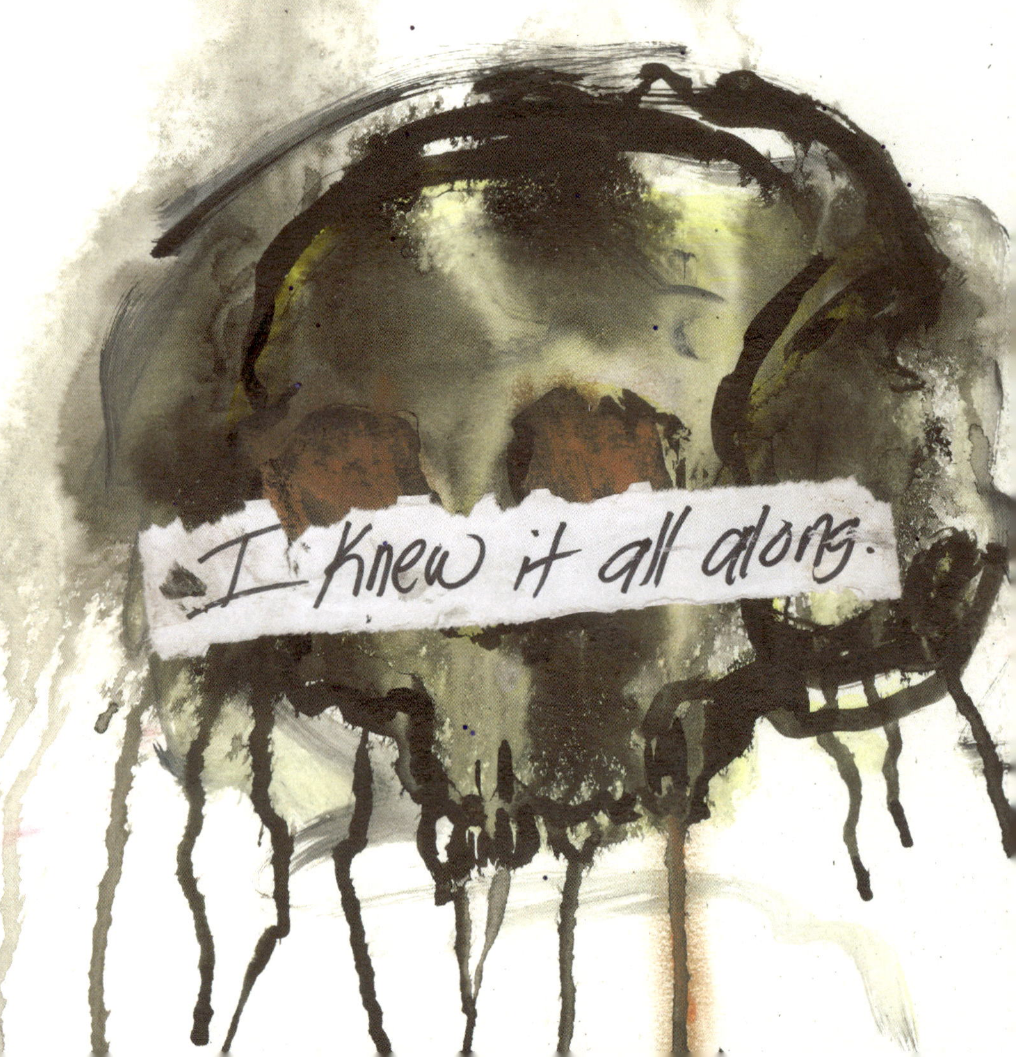
I'm in disbelief
again.
I knew it all along.

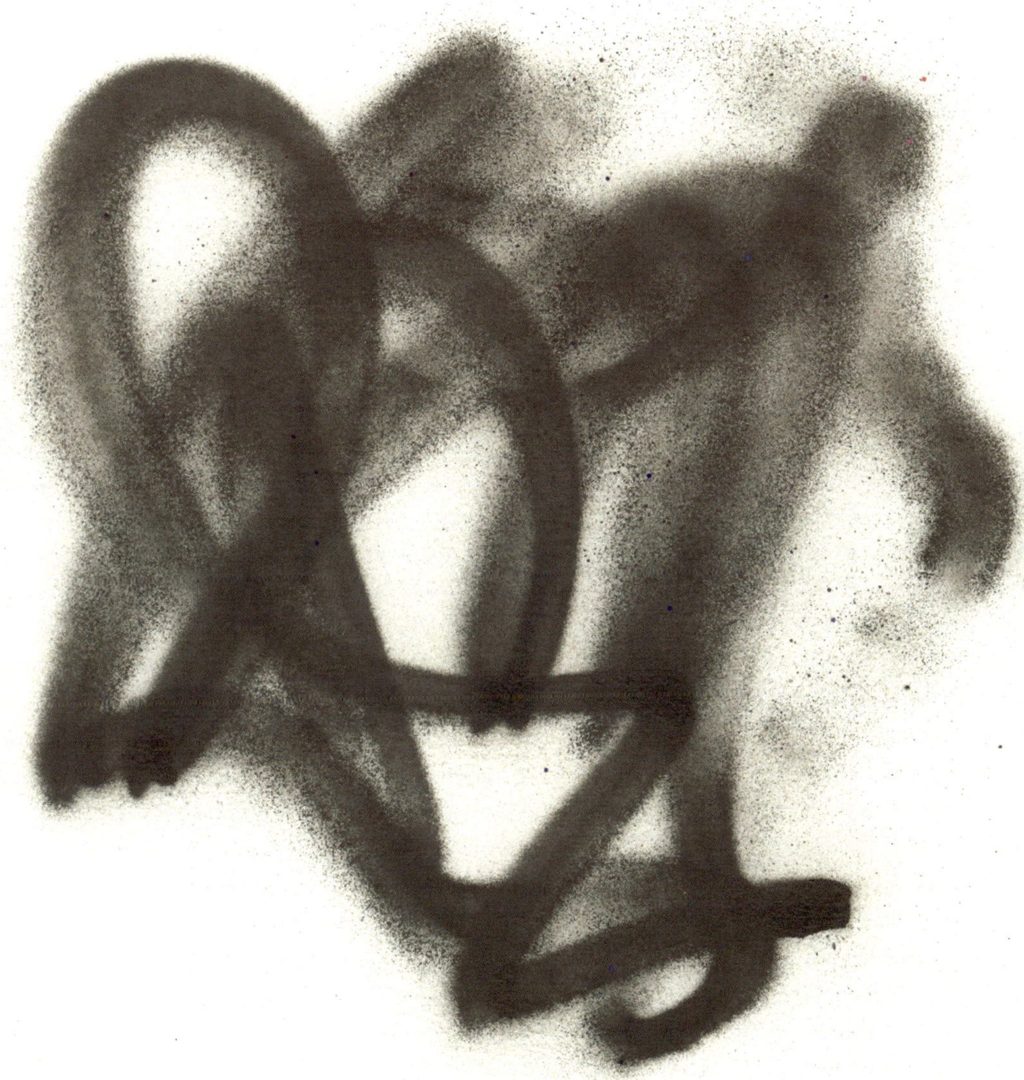

this isn't happening.

Were those
pills a metaphor   overtimed   He
Pulling a   wen
Stuck in 1999.   never
Did you   Are you   wanted   had
loose   reading this?   family   enough
use me?
   thread   Did he   He
your success   doesn't
may be stagnant. Kill his father.   have
   takes   He said I   enough
your husband
wanted to fuck didn't   why did
                                    you have
Patience   a child

But I   He is a rabbit   He said
left when fucking   He
    out of the rattle
I had enough.   ...what was
                        fantasy.

To not have my
animosity means that
I no longer keep
my eye.

PISS
OFF

the ▪▪ days ▪▪re burning
into each other. Are they
barreling into a new future? We
what do other people do are
when they see the after all
word fatel? De
may ▪▪▪▪ to
then? I sie
are for w   I
fed weight free.
difference   s
can receive. I can relish
in weight that is mine.

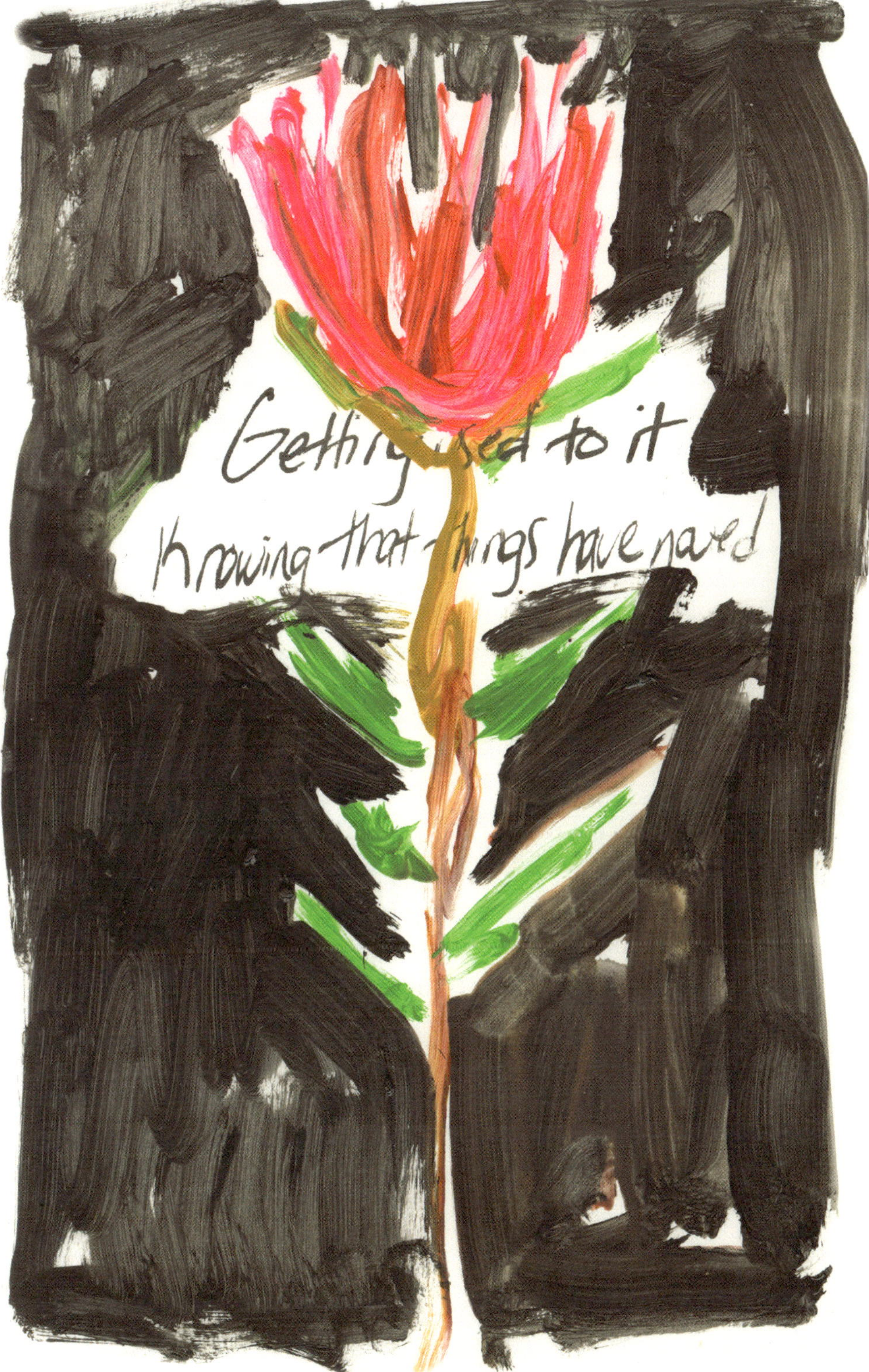

Getting used to it
Knowing that things have naked

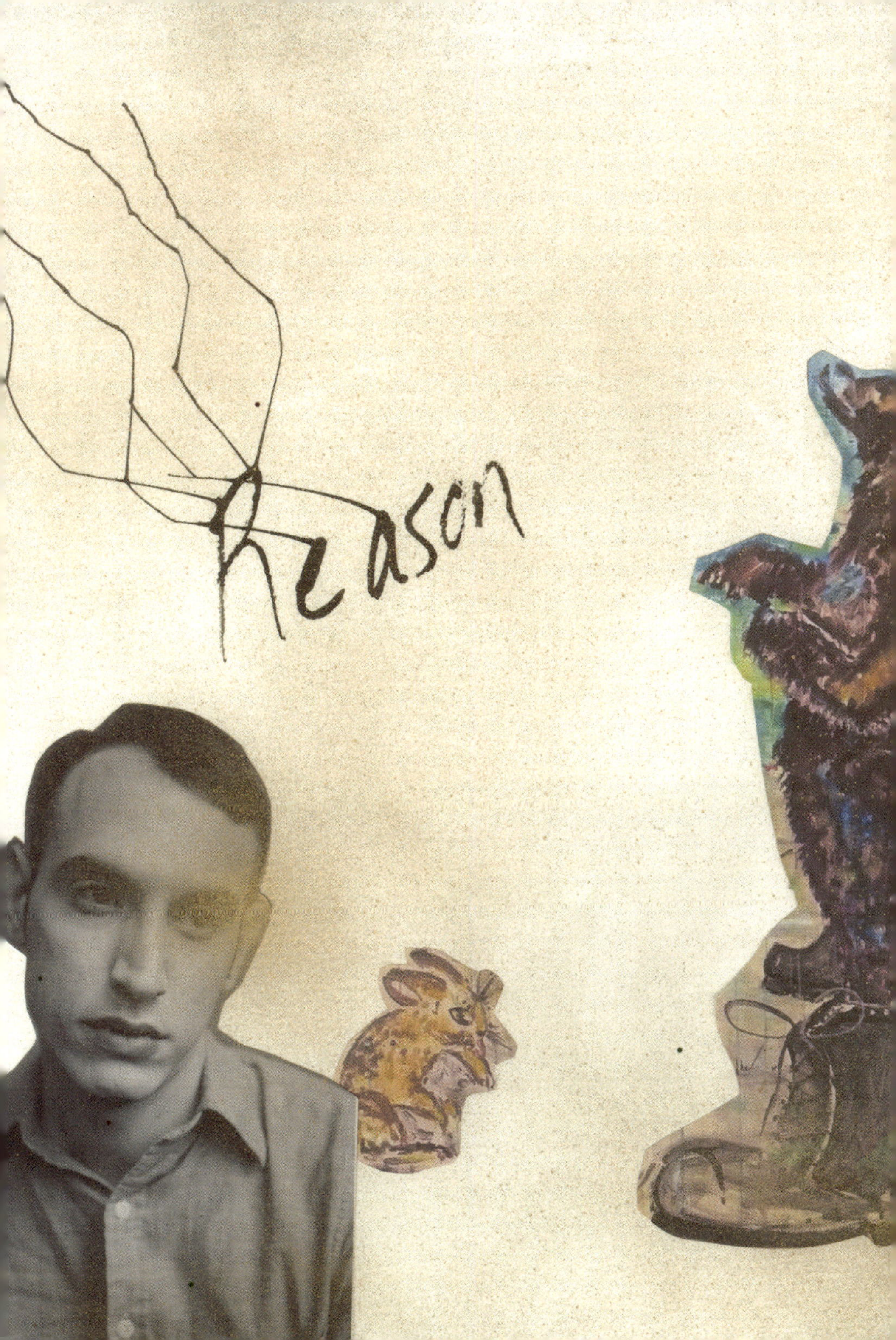
reason

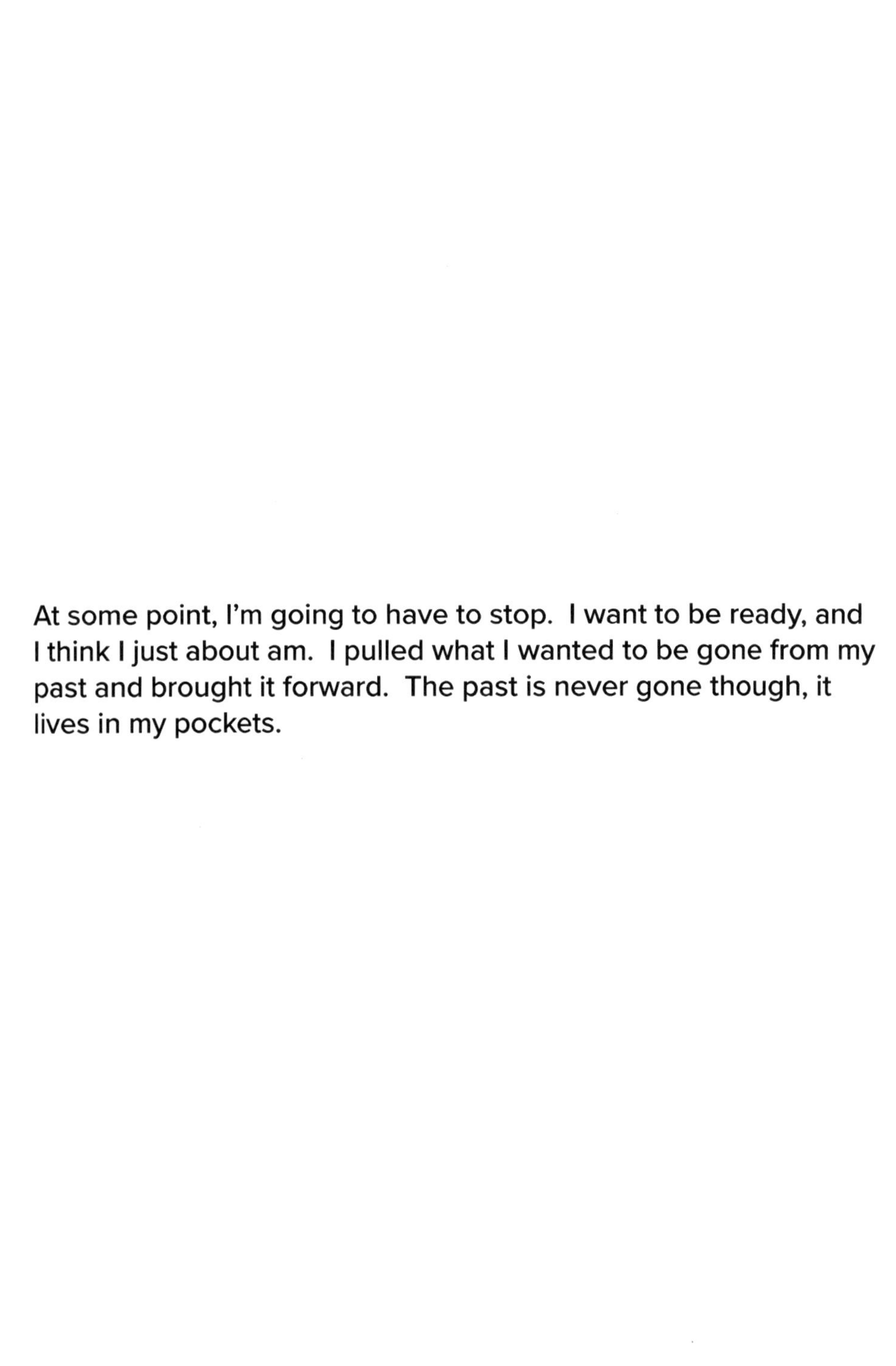

At some point, I'm going to have to stop. I want to be ready, and I think I just about am. I pulled what I wanted to be gone from my past and brought it forward. The past is never gone though, it lives in my pockets.

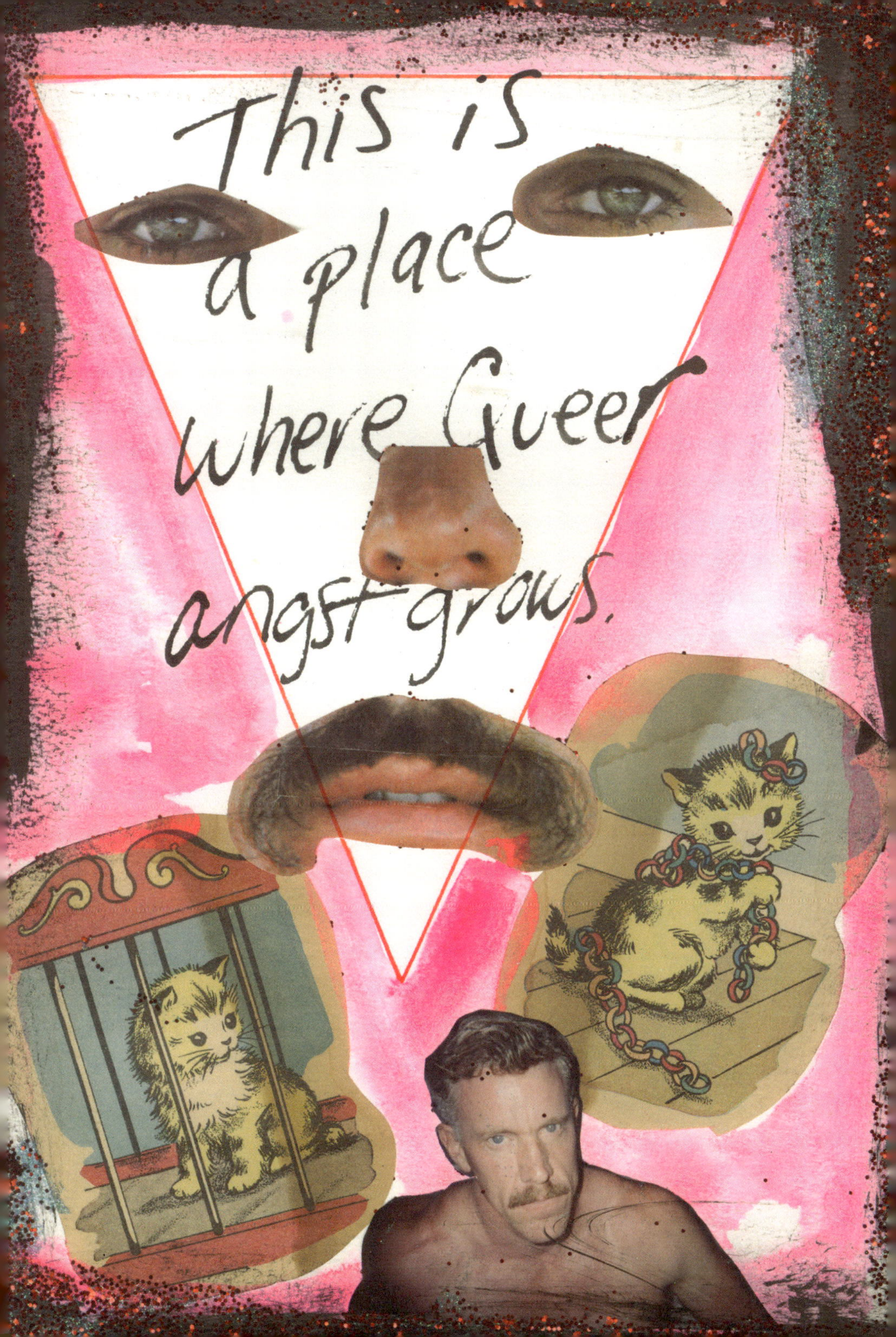

This is
a place
where Queer
angst grows.

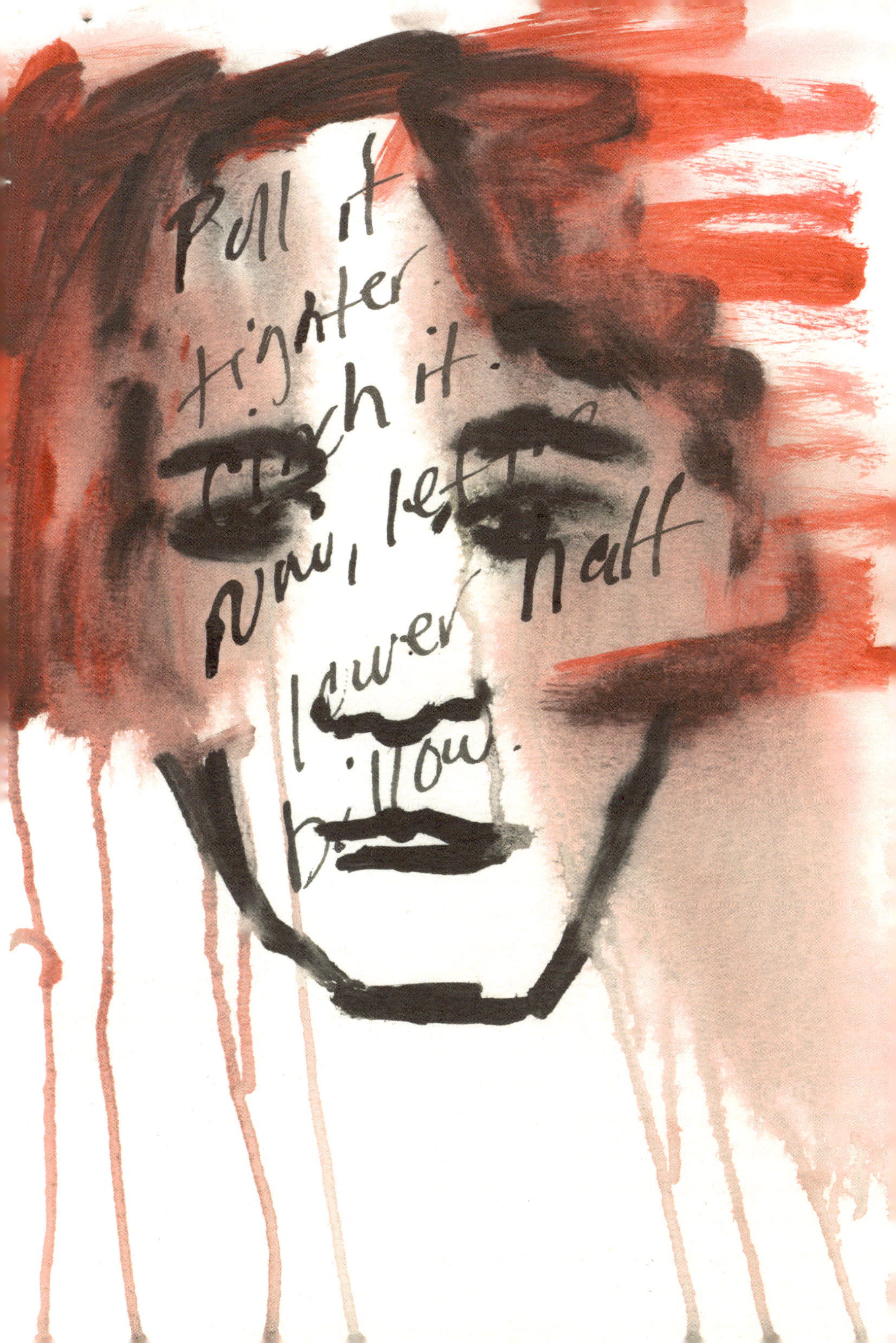

Pull it
tighter.
Cinch it.
Now, let
lower half
billow.

this
i saw where
the fantastical
becomes
REAL

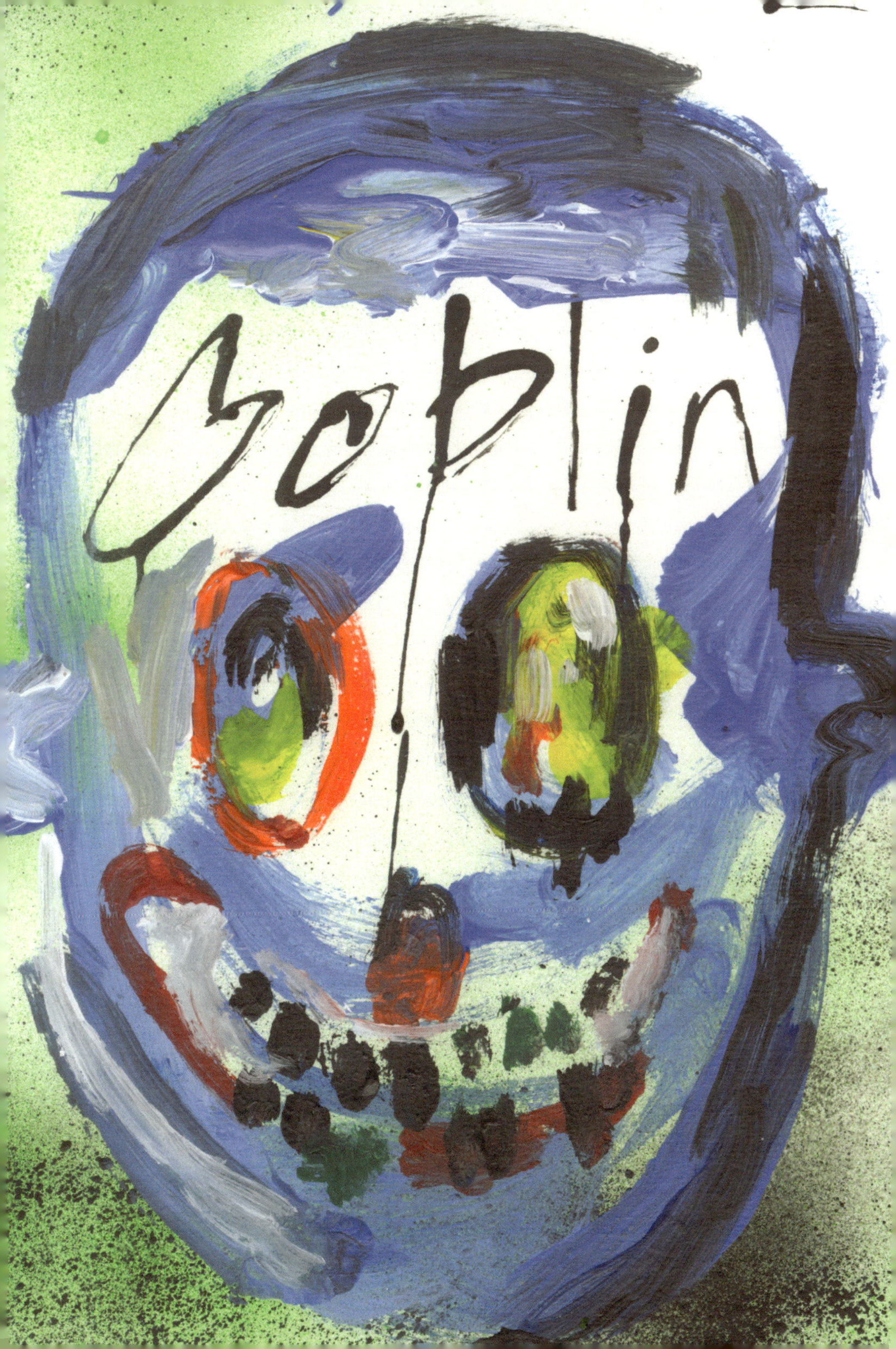

Goblin

I was waiting
for him to come

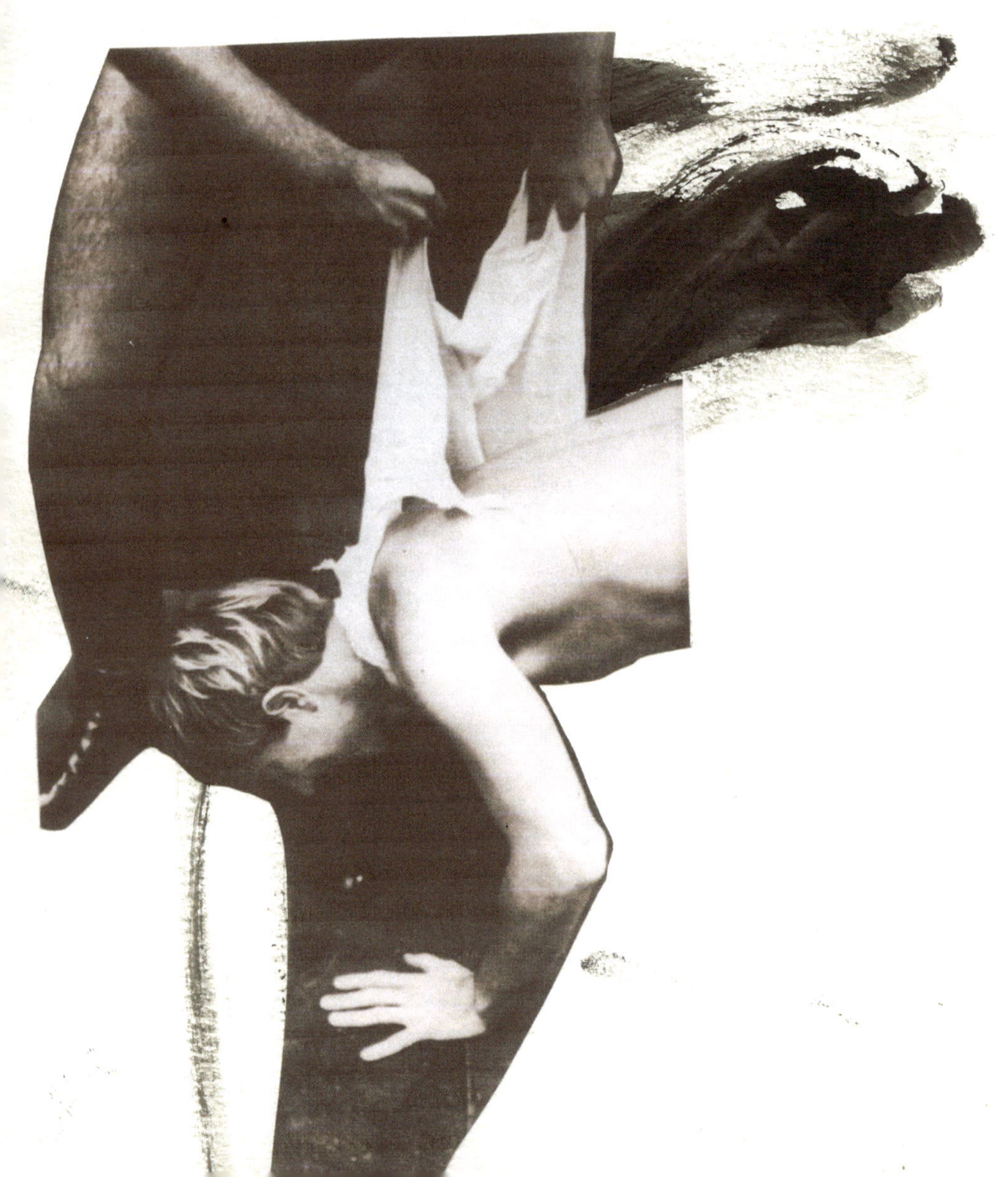

I knew he
would not
be in the
form of a
father

I asked
myself, is
he seeing
through me?
911 TRAIN

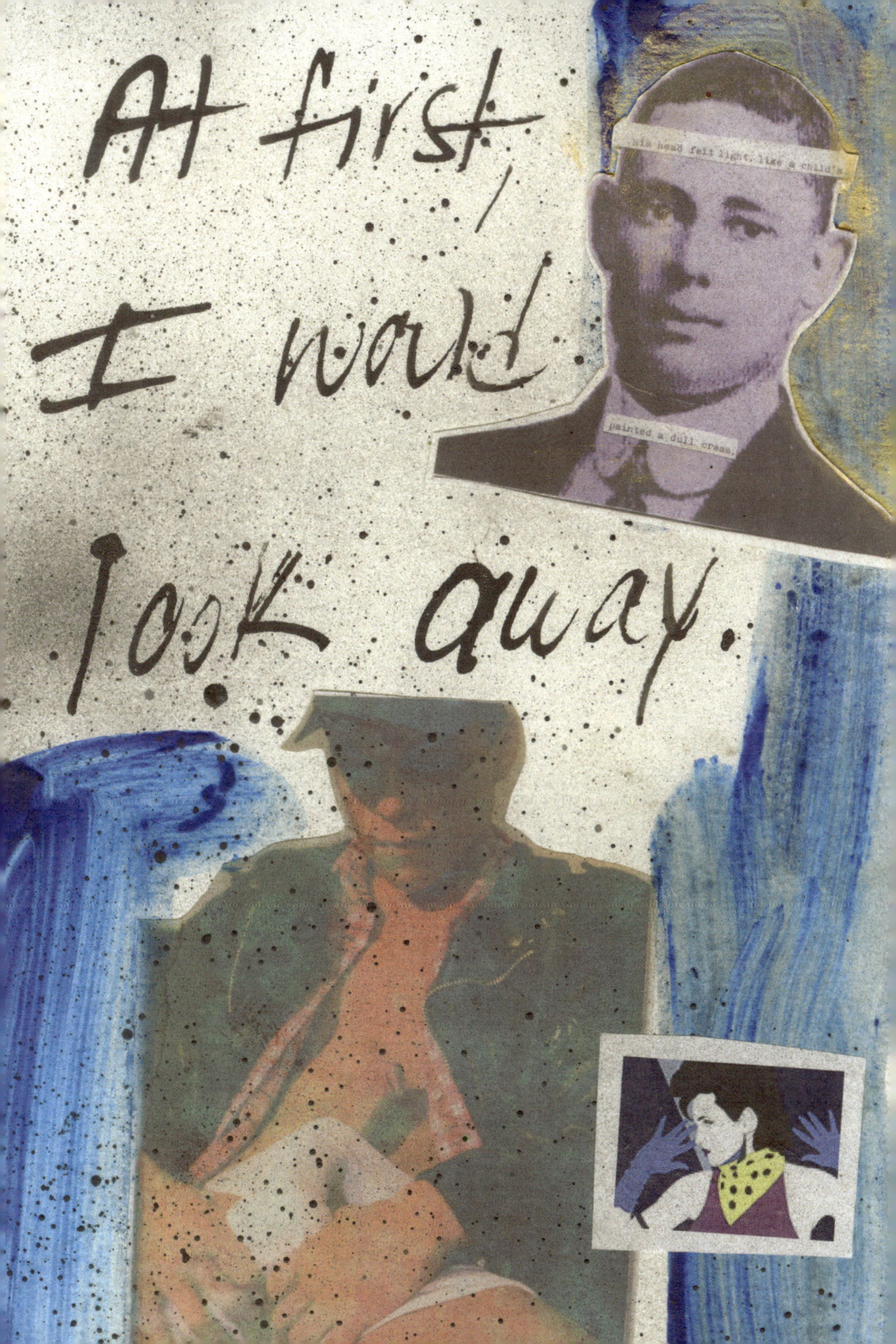
At first,
I would
look away.
his head felt light, like a child's.
painted a dull cream,

His stare was too piercing.
Like I said, I thought he was seeing through me.
But he wasn't.
He was giving me his gift.

His horns are not evil or even particularly sharp.
His horns are a birthright.
I had to jump.
He gave me the courage to jump.
And what happens when I jump?

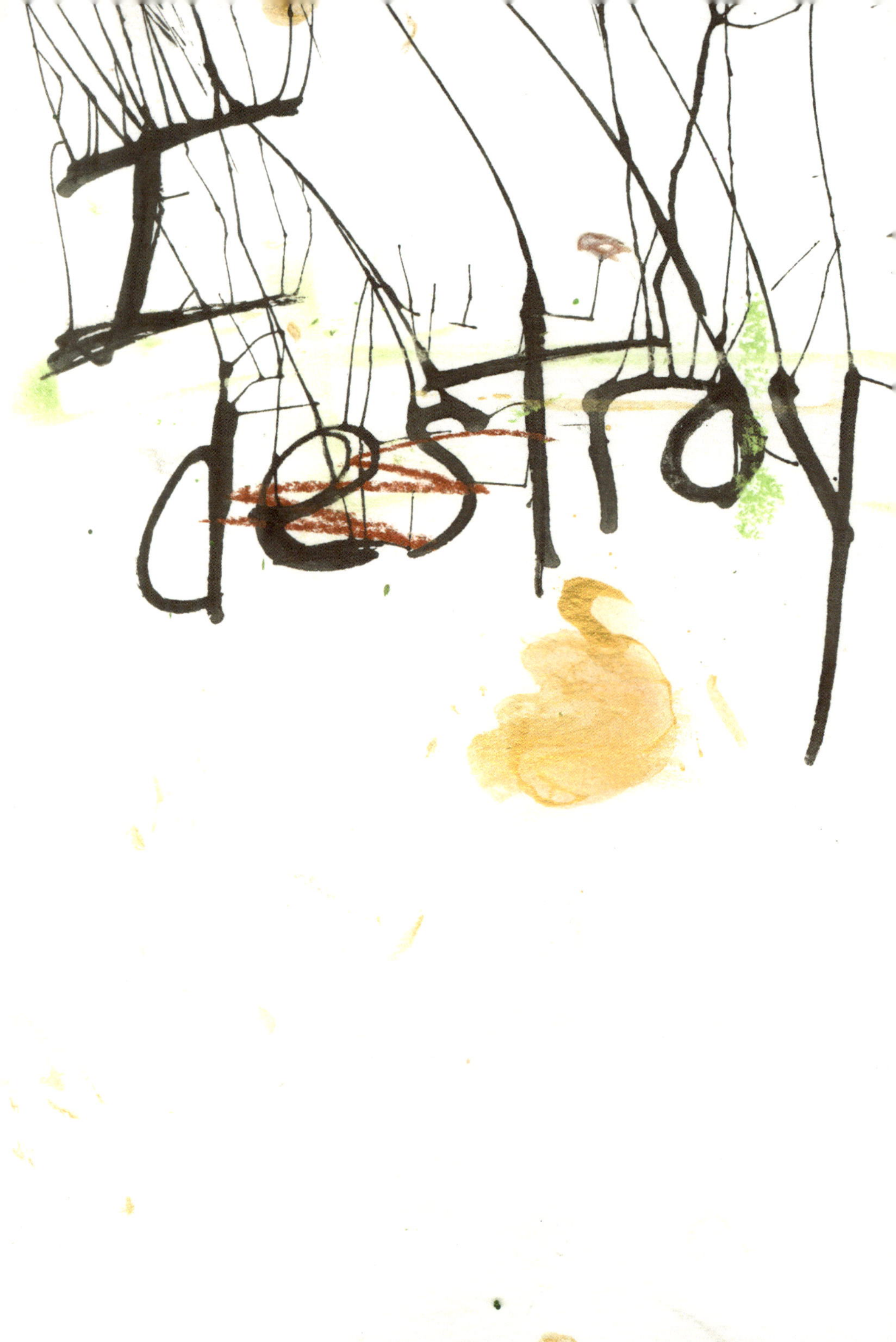

I destroy

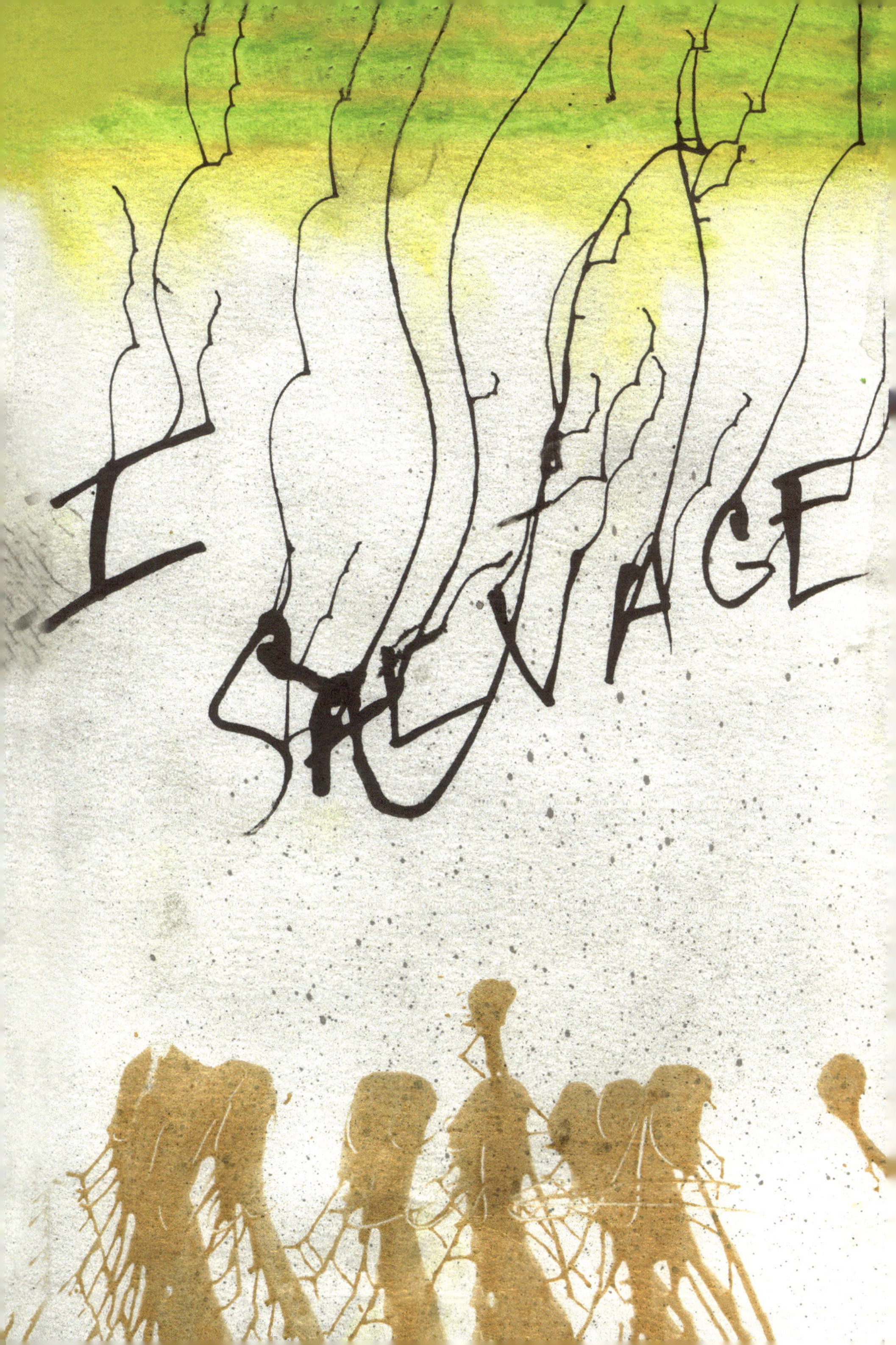

I SAUVAGE

I knew last night was the night I'd do it.
I broke the barriers. I did what I was warned not to do.
I felt the hairs on a boy's legs against mine. Finally, I tempted him.
I got too drunk, I took too many shots.

I wanted to be fucked as I made my way to a sex shop where a
stranger fed me poppers and cleaned my ass with wipes, like a
baby.

It wasn't enough.

I smoked from a stranger's pipe and said things that I cannot share.

Others may not understand.

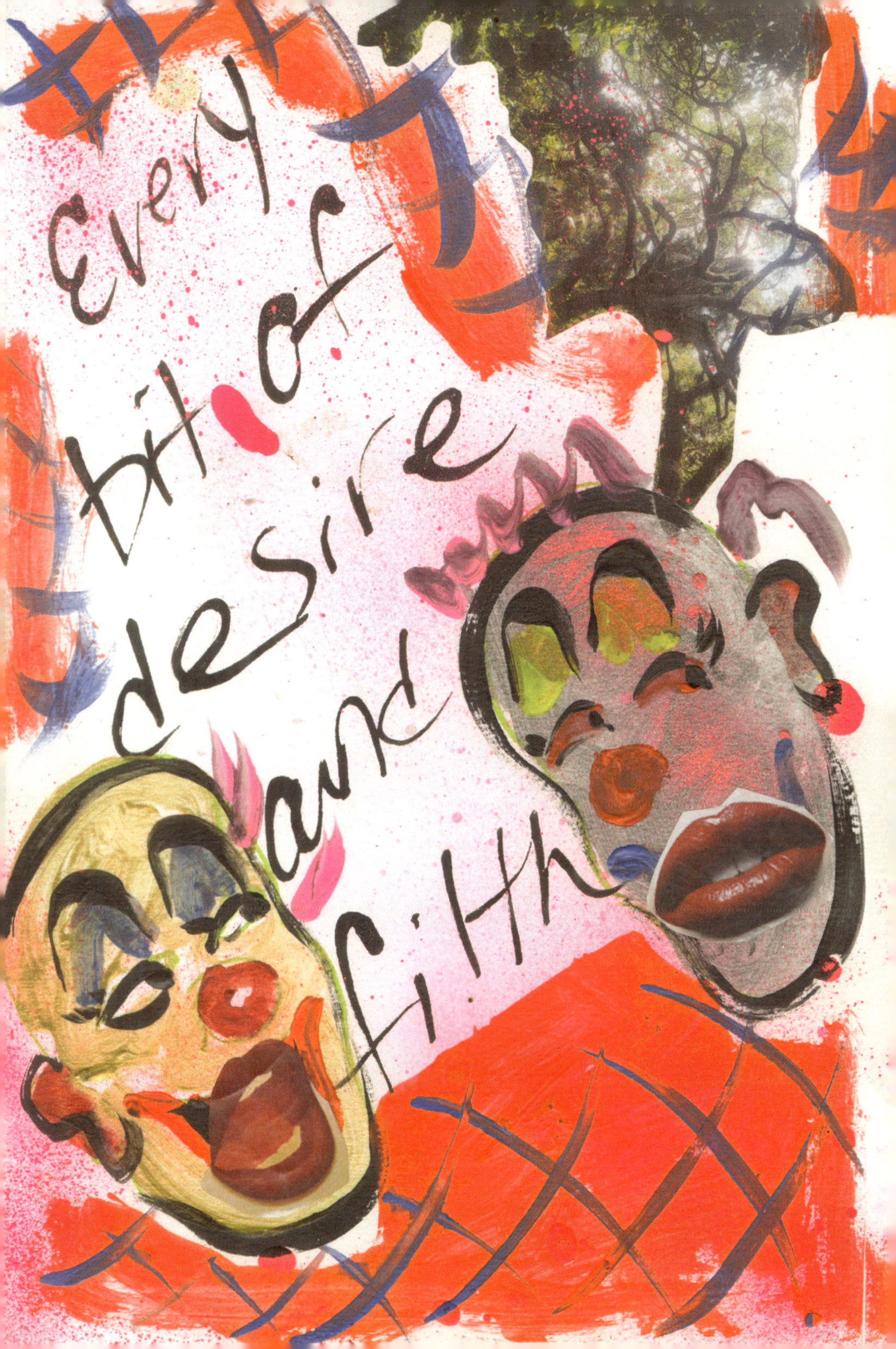

Every
bit of
desire
and
filth

Pent up for weeks, months, years, years, and years.

I sought someone down the street, it was already past dawn.
I wasn't attracted to him, not when I sucked his dick, nor when I sucked and licked his hole.
But I had a job to do.
No, not the one I called out from, not a 9-5.

When my neighbor let me inside his home, I laid him down and pushed myself into his ass, his warm, slippery ring.

I asked, "Do you like Daddy fucking you? Do you remember when we first did this?"

He moaned
Daddy
said
I
share
"Don't apologize," he said.

I watched two middle-aged men jerk their fat, grown cocks that I made him pull up on his cell phone.

It was how I stayed hard, it was how I was able to remain inside him, fucking him.

This stranger, this boy, this man, my neighbor.

I cahn't
curr in him
not like
he wants

WHAM-O
celebs flee

I jerked what was left of me onto his face.
He jumped when I smacked my dick against his tongue.

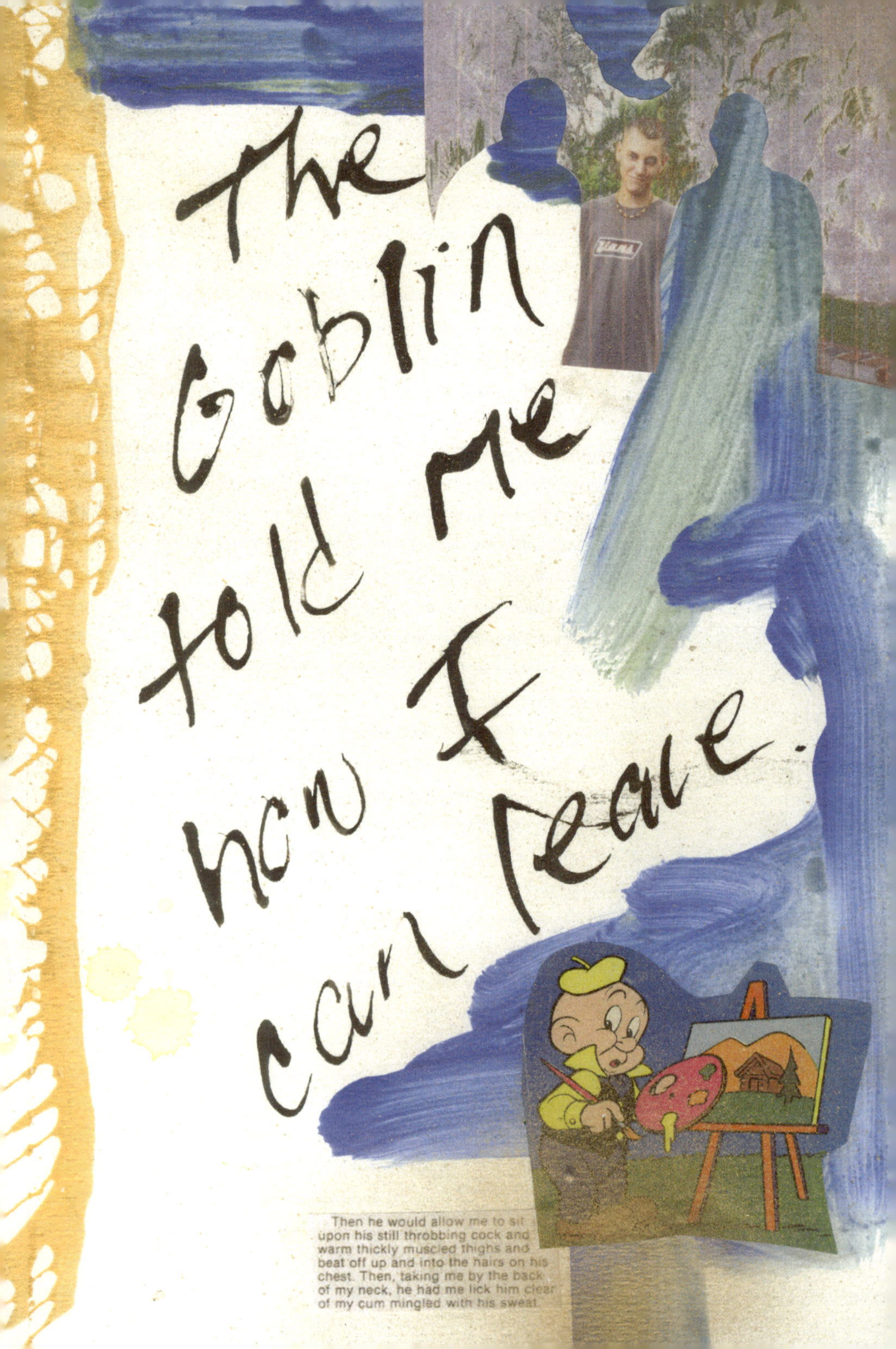
The Goblin told Me how I can Peare.
Then he would allow me to sit
upon his still throbbing cock and
warm thickly muscled thighs and
beat off up and into the hairs on his
chest. Then, taking me by the back
of my neck, he had me lick him clear
of my cum mingled with his sweat.

He gave me a way out,
out of this machine,
out of the clog,
out of the ego.

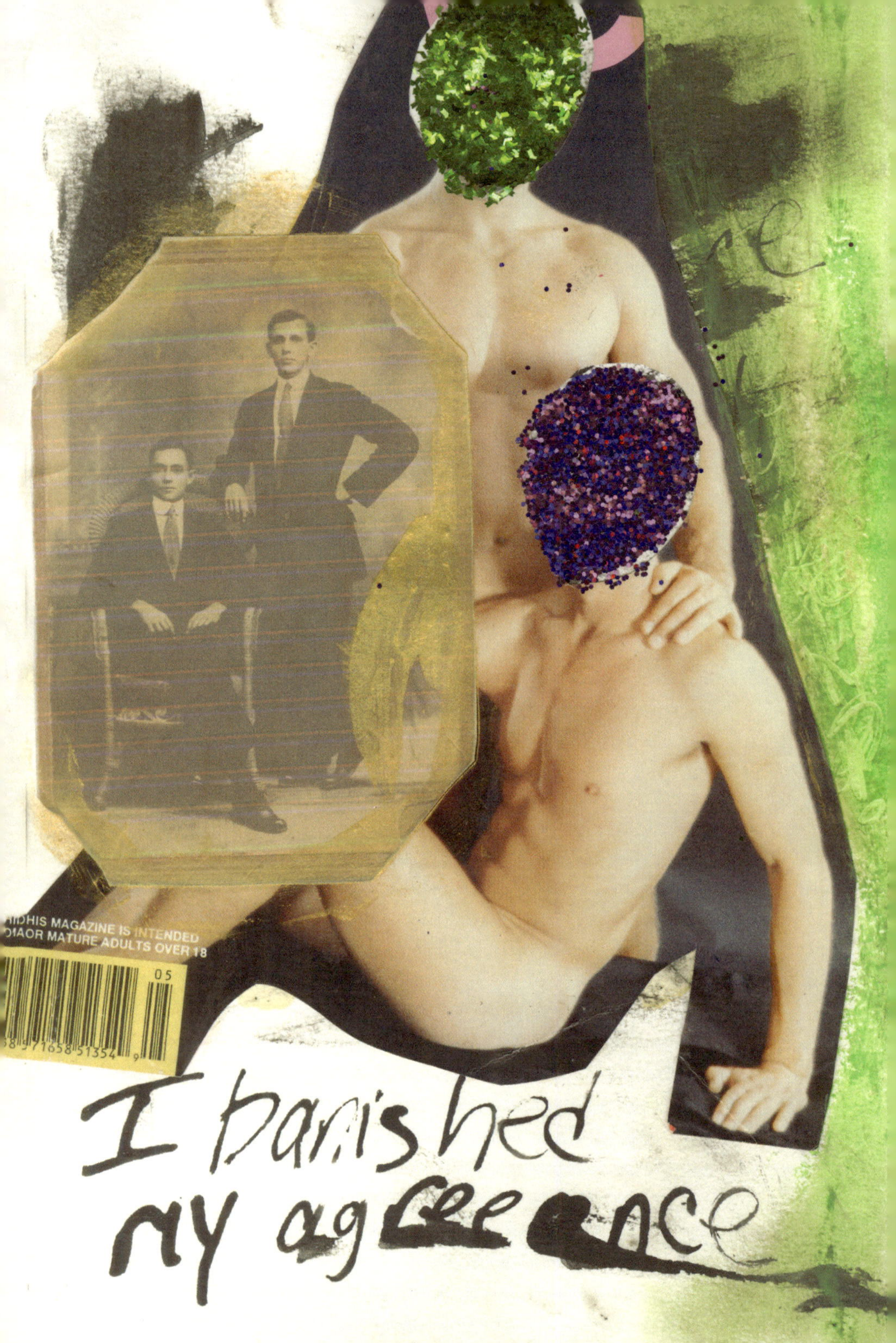
THIS MAGAZINE IS INTENDED FOR MATURE ADULTS OVER 18
05
I banished my agreeance

I banished my conflict of wanting to appease others
and also, to grind them down.

This man,
this monster,
this Goblin, who came to me with his knubby, green horns and his perfect stare was not a part of my home or my past.

The Goblin showed me how to escape, escape from my mundane.
Now I wonder, how long will he dance with me?
That question doesn't matter, you see.
It doesn't matter because time stops when he stares at me, giving
me his gift every time we are about to part.

me
and you
are
suspended
in time.

Raunchy
my
Goblin
POSH
liquid SPANISH FLY
the REAL THING
SUMMER
my
Goblin
Pythagoras

A fresh grave in the
yard; being touched like
a Sofia Coppola montage,
a smiling sweet man, an
affable Goblin, a repair,
a memory, Diane Keaton
died today, variations and
hard wiring of the past
neither cared And Kitten
if they can see is thrash
our windows, have it be.

I know that there
isn't an ending.
I fool myself into
thinking that there
is.

over and over
and over again.

What will it feel like to feel
my husband's body again? I
miss him like how one misses their
home. I'd like to be underneath
a heap of blankets, my heels taching
his legs. The care I feel for
him is enough.

Your
tone
was
sweet.
You
laid
voice
to what
is new.
I hope he receives it.

There
was a
~~Done of~~
of want
wanting

An open love
letter.
Sneaky pliant, hidden messages and hesitance
that inspires jealousy.

"Are you okay?" asked the artist.
"Yea, I'm fine."
"I'm probably projecting," he said.
"I'm good. Are you ok?"
"I'm good."

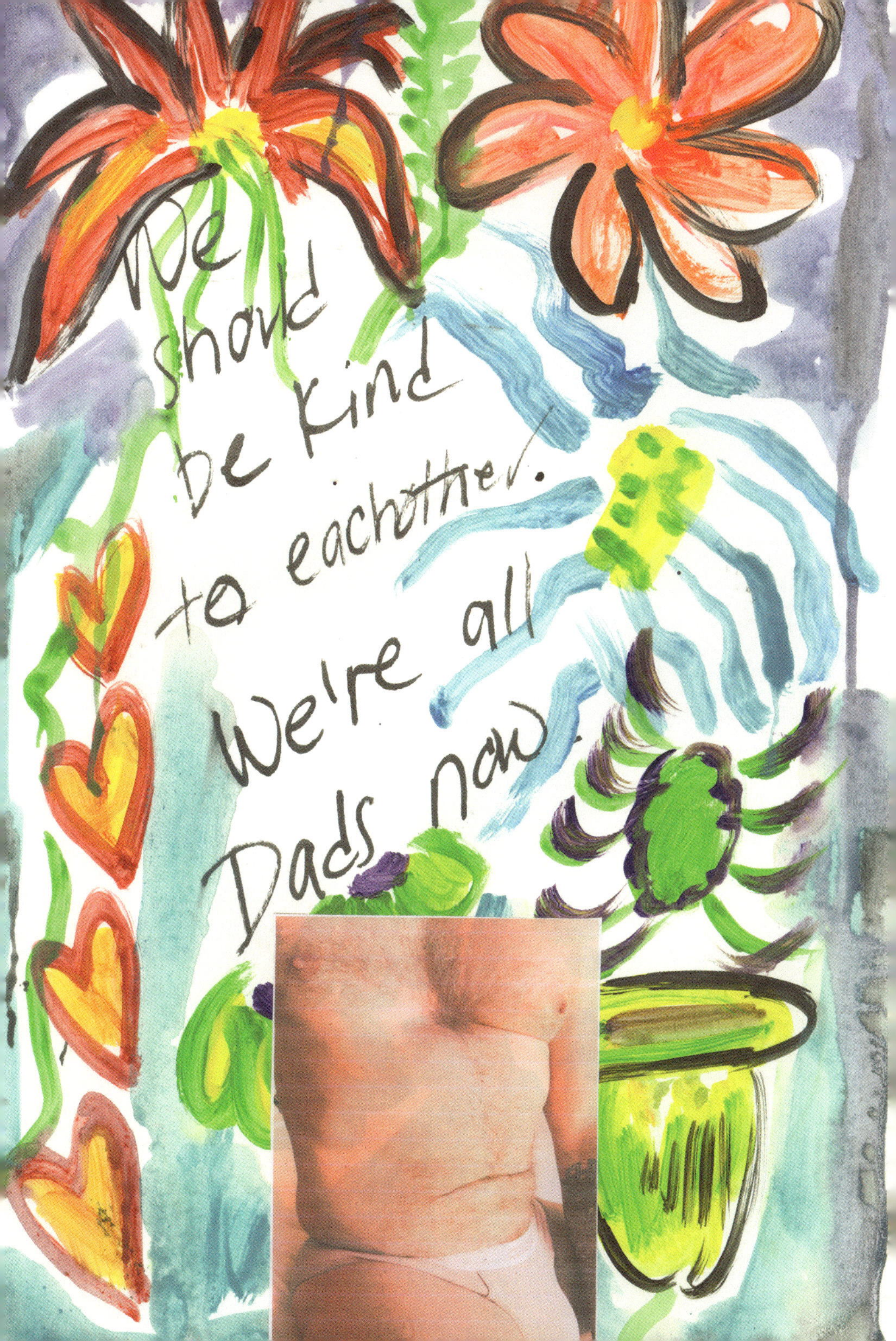

We
should
be kind
to eachother.
We're all
Dads now.

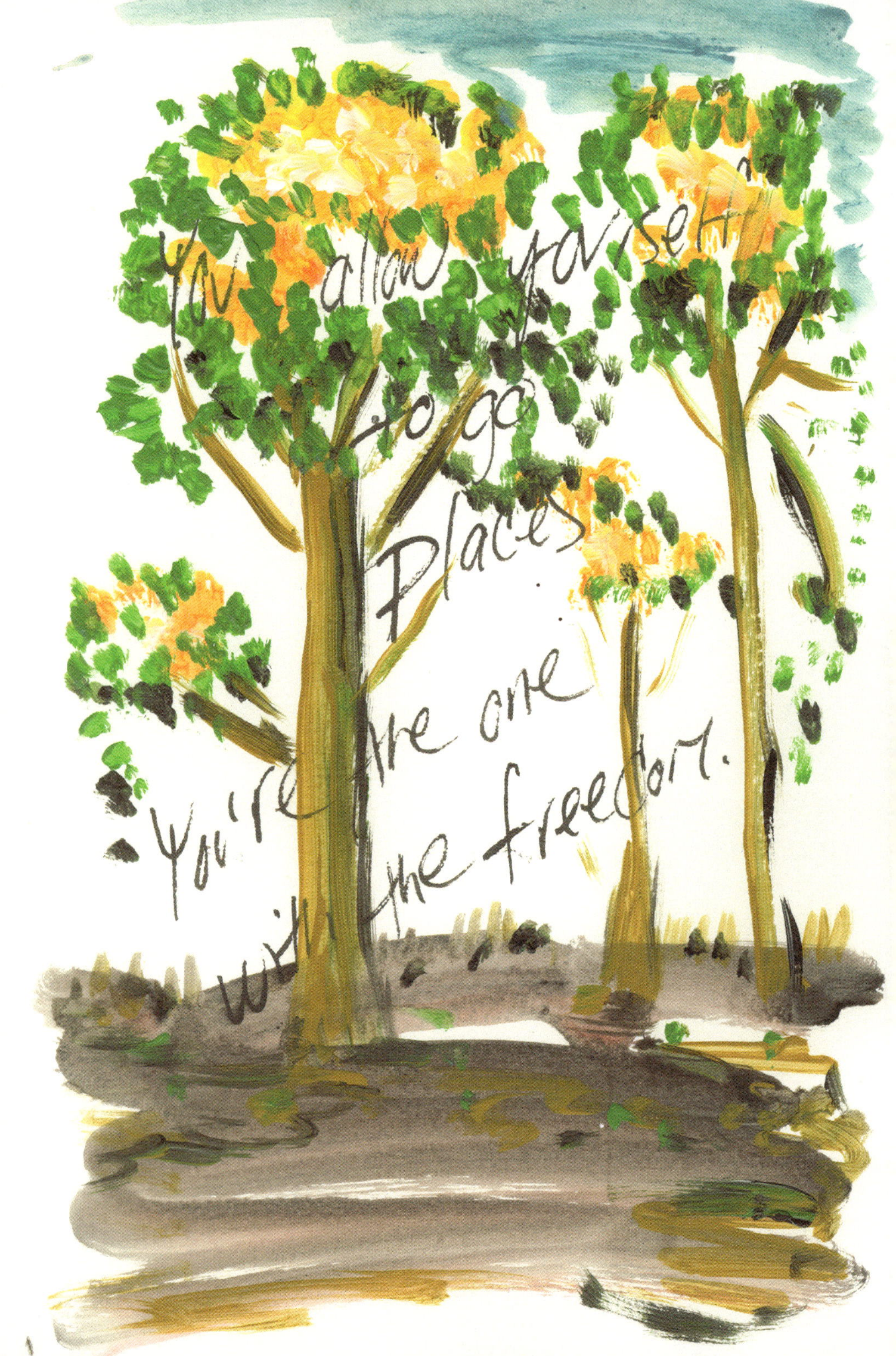

You allow yo'self to go
Places
You're the one
with the freedom.

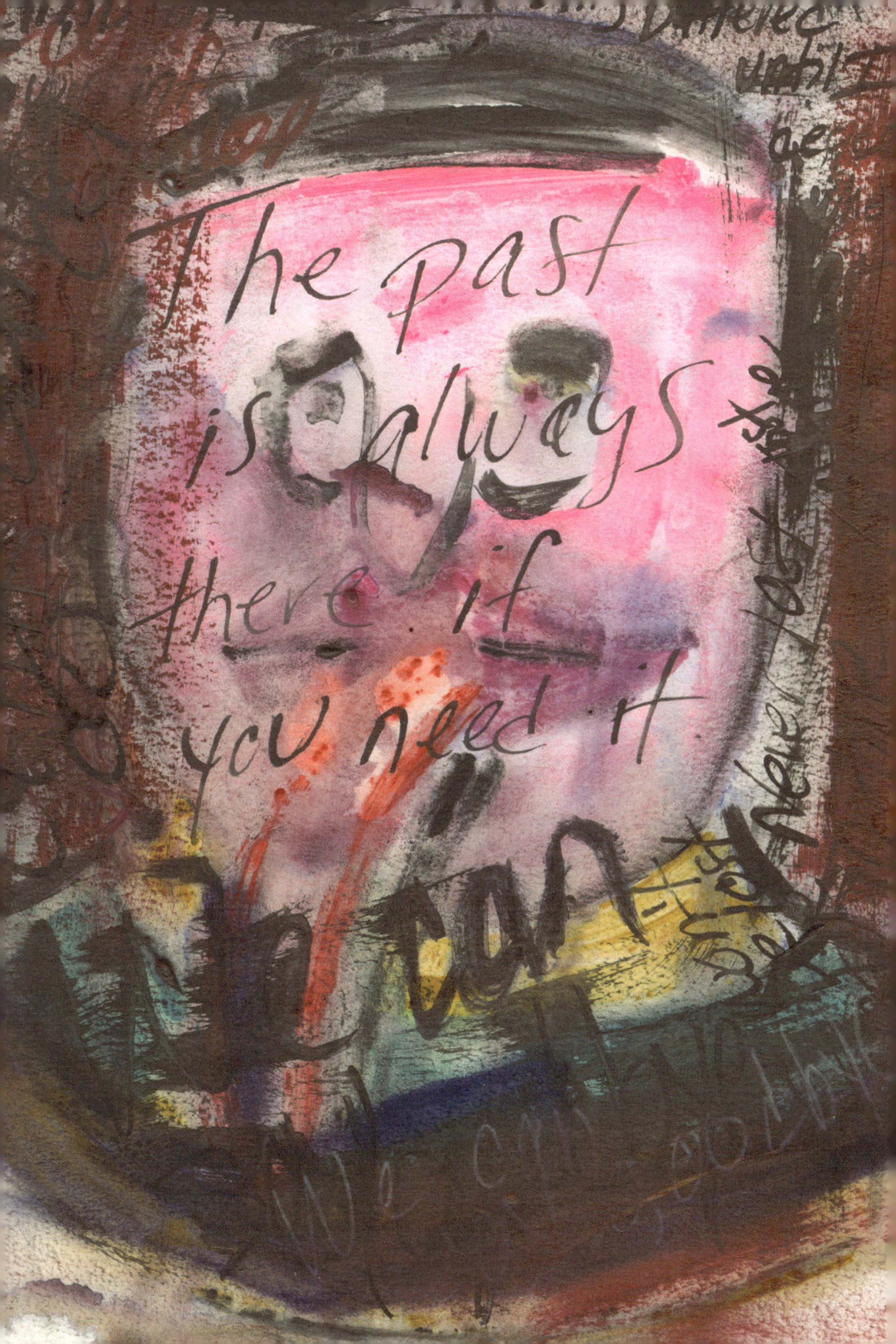

The past
is always
there . if
you need it

Response By
Nate Lippens

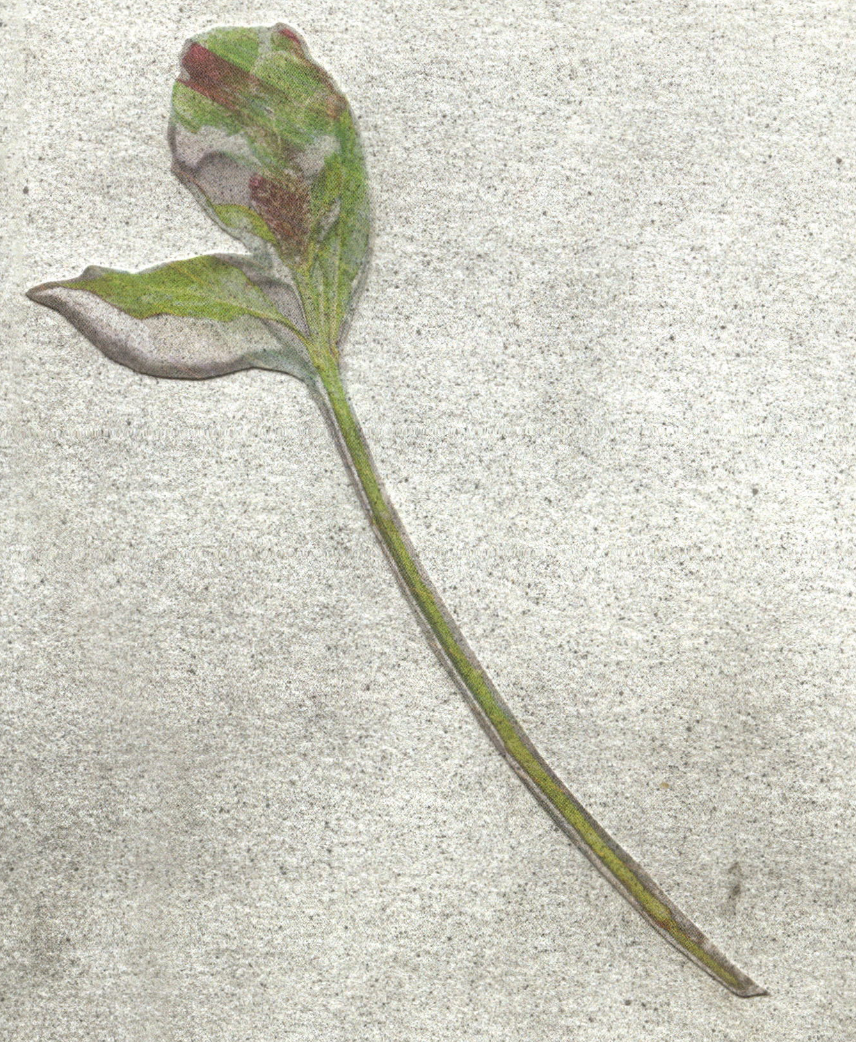

Signed, Sealed, Undelivered
Nate Lippens

Frontage Road or Frottage Row as some called it because of all the standup action. No one wanted to kneel, no one wanted to bend, so they stood and rubbed cocks, pulled out like hibernated animals emerging after the long winter. Pale, hungry, abrupt.

Darling crooned the radio of a parked car. Ambience.

I wanted to get home, an odd instinct because I didn't have one. I lived by the good graces and sleazy motivations of others. Crash pads, sublets, a back porch, a spare room, a new friend's couch. Alert to the mood shifts, the small gestures, eye contact. I knew how to time my exits.

A mohair sweater with patchy flat spots, cowlicks of wear. A gift from a Chicago man passing through. Bird on a breeze, unnoticed, above it all.

Wildness in an instant. They came and went. Back to real lives. These moments were the IOUs to people they couldn't stay on earth and be.

My bus arrived either early or very late, and I took my place.

In the trailer before Mister returned from work, I stood before a steamed mirror. A rock salt face appeared and ate every story. My reflection got it all wrong, *Baby, I'm not…*

Aware of not using too much hot water, taking too long, even alone there. Shame was the beauty I woke to, clocked in to, trudged through. Mischief would cackle up at some point. A theft, a burnt remark, the spark to light and torch everything. I must begin again so it could feel like magic.

Respool my mind, say the words that brought a laugh. Not too much. Chatter, Mister hated. Sometimes I slept in his bed but usually the couch. I must bide my time through bad TV and fetching beers. At 10, before the local news was read with a neutral seriousness in heavy nasal accents, he rose from his three-hour watch, turned the TV off, and ambled down the hall, no shower, straight to bed. I pulled the sheets and pillow from a chest beside the couch and arranged my makeshift bed, unsure if I wanted Mister to call my name. He didn't and soon I heard rain, hard, thunder built, and lightning exposed the room's ugliness. My fake ID on the table flashed. I'd memorized its dates and the name too. I was a map. Or a dead letter.

This is getting a little personal, but I don't mind.

Memories piled like junked cars and about as useful. Discern models and makes, sentimental attachments, the travels and detours recalled.

Now I'm garden-bearded, woolly and grayer each day. I died and came back, no savior, just stubborn. It's not as bad as I thought it would be, but I'd imagined the worst. Mary the Contrarian with plain speech that every other man thinks is a riddle. They want to understand. I know confusion is the only truth. I'm not as mean as they think. I even know some good men. That takes some doing. Real optimism. I can find the best in people as long as I stay home alone.

I spent most of my life doing things other people's way, to please and conform and get paid and have less discomfort, and now I do things how I want. No one knows what to do with me. I can't get a handle on you, a man said. How wonderful at last to be unhandled.

My room, the first down the hall. 10 x 10. The others walk by, going and coming. The sounds of lives, busied and motioned, passing. At night, slippers on tile. Someone using the bathroom. I walk around barefoot, sleep naked. Piss in a mason jar and empty it out the window.

Mrs. Day, the landlady, lives across the courtyard. Her lights go on and off, nearly morse code, but they are not a signal or communication, only a scattered mind to and fro, room to room, finding and losing things. A threshold, she said once blankly before me, I walk through a doorway and forget why I came. The rent, I said and held the check out. Yes, yes, she smiled. I did not say, what else could it be? Eviction, I suppose, but I keep my affairs quiet and pay exactly on time, never early, never late. A model tenant in my spare, clean room.

I am human...

Everybody loves a good song.

Scraped skin leaving tough terrain.

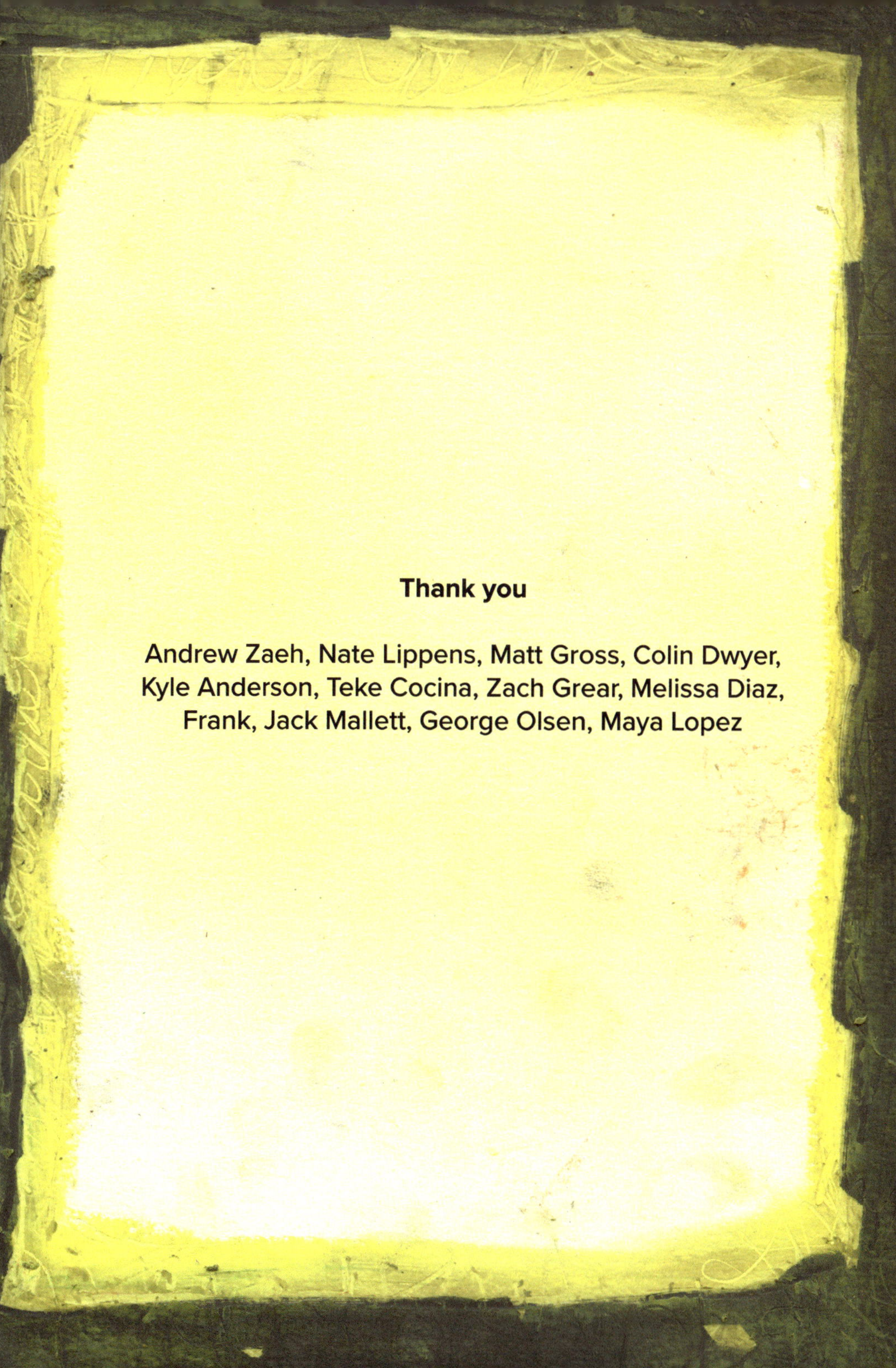

Thank you

Andrew Zaeh, Nate Lippens, Matt Gross, Colin Dwyer, Kyle Anderson, Teke Cocina, Zach Grear, Melissa Diaz, Frank, Jack Mallett, George Olsen, Maya Lopez

Jason Haaf (b. Coral Springs, Florida) is a Brooklyn-based writer and visual artist. Largely influenced by diaristic writings and memoir, Haaf utilizes intimacy and confession at its root.

His debut novel, *Harsh Cravings* (Polari Press, 2022) is a 90-day diary taking place during the summer and fall of 2020. *Can I See Your Niche?*, featuring Haaf's cut-ups and collages is published by Trapart Books, 2023. *Watchword*, a collaborative unbound art book, featuring prose and collage was published by @ND in 2023.

His writing and art has also been featured in *Truant*, edited by Nate Lippens, *Rendering Unconscious: Psychoanalytic Perspectives, Politics & Poetry* and *The Trapartisan Review* (Trapart Books), *Shower with Affection: Group Shower* (Raw Meat Collective), and *Hello Mr.* magazine.

Haaf was a recipient of the Seattle Erotic Art Fair's Foundation Award for Literary Art (2025).

Scooter LaForge (b. Las Cruces, New Mexico) is a New York–based artist who has lived and worked in the East Village for two decades. Drawing on art history and classical themes, he creates vividly contemporary works across painting, sculpture, and drawing, marked by unorthodox techniques and striking, iconic imagery.

LaForge's work has been exhibited at the Leslie-Lohman Museum in New York, the Friedrichshof Museum in Vienna, and the Spritmuseum/Absolut Art Collection in Stockholm. A feature-length documentary, *Scooter LaForge: A Life of Art* (dir. Ethan Minsker), was released in 2023, and a 30-year survey of his paintings opened at Lesley University College of Art and Design in 2024.

He also designs a celebrated line of bespoke clothing sold through Patricia Field's ArtFashion Gallery. LaForge is a recent recipient of a Pollock-Krasner Foundation grant.

Photo by
Andrew Zaeh